HALL IN THE HEART

A FIFE PARISH HALL AND ITS COMMUNITY

1914 – 2014

Jonathan Falla

with photographs by

Rodney Mountain

Published by
Stupor Mundi Books
www.stupormundibooks.wordpress.com
for Dunbog Parish Hall Trust
Fife KY14 6JF

The Trustees acknowledge grants from the Voluntary Action Fund of the Scottish Government and from Abdie & Dunbog Community Council which together made possible this publication celebrating 100 years of Dunbog Hall. They would like also to thank the author, Jonathan Falla, and the photographer, Rodney Mountain, for their time and commitment so generously given.

ISBN 978-0-9510596-2-3

First published February 2014
Corrected and expanded 2023

Text copyright © Jonathan Falla 2014 & 2023
All new photographs copyright © Rodney Mountain 2014
Others from the archives of Rev. W. Buchan
(courtesy of Eric Titterington), David Thompson, and the community.

All rights reserved. No part of this publication may be reproduced, stored in or introduced into a retrieval system, or transmitted in any form or by any means (electronic, mechanical, photocopying, recording or otherwise) without the prior written consent of the copyright holders.

**The Trust, publisher, and author welcome any
comments, corrections and additional information
which may be incorporated into future editions.
Please email glenduckie@hotmail.com**

Set by Jonathan Falla in Liberation Serif 12pt
Designed by Isabell Buenz

Contents

- 1   Dunbog: the shape of the Parish
- 8   Draining away the people
- 11   The reputation of the people
- 16   1864: the Dunbog Gunpowder Plot
- 20   1910-14: Before the building of the Hall
- 23   Who built Dunbog Hall – and why?
- 27   The Hall is begun
- 32   The original Hall building
- 35   Putting the new Hall to use
- 37   1914-18: The Great War in Dunbog
- 40   1918-30: Uneasy with the peace
- 43   1930: Out of control
- 49   World War 2 and other distractions
- 53   Women's shadows
- 57   Crackles on the line
- 62   1945-52: Taking the Hall back for the Parish
- 65   1954: a new Deed of Trust
- 66   Dunbog in the early 1950s
- 69   1954: Tentative expansion
- 72   1955-67: The doldrums
- 77   1967-99: Staying alive
- 87   2000: Millenium rebirth
- 93   The Path
- 94   Dunbog 2014 and beyond
- 101   A Community Park
- 102   Bibliography, sources and acknowledgements

HALL IN THE HEART

The Parish Hall of Dunbog was built in 1914. It is not an especially glamorous building, nor is it part of a picture-book village. Dunbog Hall sits unadorned beside a main road, next to a modern house and an 1830s primary school. Otherwise, the nearest buildings are a row of cottages some few hundred yards along that road. Distant farms and more clumps of cottages, and the Victorian spire on a Georgian kirk can be glimpsed from the hall, but there is no village as such. This is a small, scattered rural community that has gone through many changes, has lost a great deal of population in recent centuries, and has never been rich.

The story of the hall provides an intriguing window on life in a Scottish country parish over a century or more. This story illustrates many of the hardships that such communities have faced, the tensions in society, the difficulties caused by those who would control it from outside – and, on occasion, a few triumphs too.

But we should start by looking at the human and physical landscape in which the hall was built.

Dunbog: the shape of the parish

Dunbog, in north-east Fife, is today barely half an hour's drive from Perth, Dundee, Glenrothes, or St Andrews. But for much of its history, this was an obscure part of the world. Even the name was uncertain: Dunbulc, Dinbog, Dunbolg, Doumboug, Dynbug, and other variants may all be met.[1] The parish almost overlooks the Tay, but not quite: it is cut off from the water by wooded hills reaching some 700 feet, and only a little tongue of land ever touched the river. Hills nearly enclose the parish, and from the tops one can see Dundee and the Tay bridges to the east, and the outskirts of Perth to the west, with the Central Highlands and

---

[1] Many of these are examined in Taylor (2010) and on Glasgow University's Fife Place-names database. The first record of the name *Dunbulc* is from 1189.

Schiehallion beyond. From most of the cottages and farms, however, the view is restricted to fields and wooded slopes, the A913, and – at night – the orange light pollution seeping up from distant towns. So, if the parish is hardly cut off, it is more circumscribed and defined than the scattered homes might suggest.

Norman's Law

People and societies have passed through, leaving their marks. On Norman's Law and Glenduckie Hill are traces of Iron Age fortified settlements, and *c*.210 CE the inhabitants would have watched apprehensively as a Roman army built a large camp at Carpow, just beyond Newburgh; it was an expedition led by the Emperor Severus, intent on exterminating the tribes to the north, but it would have begun by 'pacifying' communities in nearby Fife. Just over the ridge, on the Tay coast, Ballinbreich castle was in the Middle Ages the home of great lords, but it is now a ruin glimpsed among trees by the water. William Wallace is supposed to have fought a skirmish somewhere down there,[2] and Mary Queen of Scots stayed a night or two in the castle at Collairnie which today is decrepit and has a concrete silage tower next door, built to much the same height and colour, and given amusing battlements in the baronial spirit.

The kirk has come and gone from Dunbog and the hamlet of Glenduckie;[3] that name possibly honours a Scottish saint, Duthac.[4] There are records from 1189 of an ancient chapel – *capella de Dunbulc* – overlooking the Tay near Bankside, but the archaeologists are not sure where it was. There was another chapel out in a field by the Denmuir lane, but it is now overgrown; most people glancing that way from the main road and seeing a clump of trees have no idea that there's a ruin in the middle. In Dunbog lane there was a kirk beside the graveyard; a branch-office of Arbroath Abbey here was staffed by four monks.[5] Later, a mansion called Dunbog House was built on the site. A 1980s guide book to Fife[6] mentions the house and says that it is 'much altered'. Indeed so: it was slowly demolished between 1952 and 1969, having been semi-derelict for years. Only a gable end now stands among a tangle of greenery. The kirk was replaced in 1803 by a new building, with a spire added in 1888, but this kirk too is closed, and is used as a private residence.

What else? The economy has been mostly agricultural, but many villages in north Fife were once occupied by handloom weavers; flax grew well in Fife, and weaving linen was the economic main-

---

[2] The Battle of Black Earnside. The exact location is uncertain, as is the date, variously given as 1298 or 1304. It may have been little more than a skirmish.

[3] Strictly speaking, Glenduckie lies in the parish of Flisk. But Flisk is over the hill, and for most practical purposes Glenduckie is regarded as part of Dunbog.

[4] Taylor (2010) has no time for St Duthac, but offers no firm alternative. East Cottage, Glenduckie, was formerly called 'Duthac'.

[5] The 'Preceptory of Gadvan'. It may have been administering the abbey's lands in the area.

[6] *Fife in History & Legend* by Raymond Lamont-Brown (1988, reprinted 2002). There are myths about this mansion: that it was built by Cardinal Bethune who burned martyrs at St Andrews, or perhaps by another Cardinal for a mistress. Neither is true. Another romantic account, *Right Royal Friend* by Nigel Tranter (2003), has King James VI hunting deer with trusty companions on Glenduckie and Ayton Hills.

Dunbog House c.1950, shortly before demolition began, with trees growing out of the windows at the far end which was used as a store by a market gardener.

stay of Newburgh; much of the fine linen produced went to Germany.

There are traces of this in our parish. On the north slope of Glenduckie Hill, among the trees close to the Fife Coastal Path is a ruined settlement of several cottages with the delightful name of Mountflowery, recorded as having been occupied by weavers. Linen weaving was hard work for small profit, involving whole families as the children helped with soaking and beating the flax – some locally grown – which the women would then spin and the men would weave. Or they would obtain linen yarn from Dundee by walking twelve miles or more to the south side of the Tay and crossing in small boats. For some families it would be winter work, when there was little to do on the land, and no fishing. It is probable that many of the smaller homes and ruins scattered throughout the parish – on the slopes of Norman's Law, for instance – were the homes of poor weavers. To support the trade, the Government passed a law requiring (on pain of quite substantial fines) that all the dead must be buried wrapped in linen cloth.

Dunbog Kirk, *c.*1950. Now a private home.

But as industrial power looms became widespread in the mid-1800s, and as American cotton and Indian jute were far cheaper and faster to process, the returns from cottage handloom weaving of linen declined rapidly until by 1890 it was almost vanished as an occupation.

The weavers' cottages at Mountflowery are shown on the Ordnance Survey map of 1855 as occupied, with a well, neat gardens and an access road. On the 1896 OS map, they have lost their roofs, are unoccupied, and the gardens and track have disappeared.

There was a commercial whinstone quarry up behind Glenduckie, and in 1857 the *Fifeshire Journal* reported a nasty accident: thirty or forty tons of rock fell taking with it two men who miraculously survived. The quarry closed after the Second World War. Glenduckie had a shop and its own small 'Female Industrial School';[7] there was a shoemaker at Countryhills, and a joiner's premises at Sandyknowe by the crossroads – but these are all private homes now. There was a railway right through the parish but it closed in 1961, leaving numerous solidly built bridge piers and high earthen embankments at which the farmers have nibbled away to regain access to their fields. There were water mills too, but these are gone. So are the polytunnels of organic vegetables at Blinkbonny; one of the workers told me of their grief on taking a phone call ordering them to stop watering the plants they'd nurtured. Scattered about the parish are 18th century wedge-shaped doocots, but the doves have departed.

A great deal has come, and then gone. What has persisted are the farmers and the farms.

Farming was not so easy. The 1882 *Ordnance Gazetteer of Scotland* describes the land of Dunbog in splendid language: 'The rocks are mainly eruptive, and the soil in a few fields is argillaceous,[8] but mostly is a shallow rich black mould.' There is an old rhyme about these parts that puts it better:

---

[7] *Westwood's Directory* (1862). It was run by a Miss Ramsay under the patronage of the Ayton estate, which owned Glenduckie farm. Presumably this offered basic literacy and numeracy together with some practical skills.
[8] i.e. volcanic, and in a few places clayish.

Bambreich stands heich,
Higham in a howe,
Glenduckie in a gitterhole
And Moonzie on a pow.[9]

Dunbog lies between two hill ridges. These were good for sheep, but the rain running off the slopes had nowhere obvious to go; it was a gitterhole, and the lower ground was a marsh – hence one popular understanding of the name Dunbog, or 'the hill fort over the marsh.'[10] On 17th century maps[11] the morass is clearly marked extending from near Kinnaird and Inchrye in a sickle shape eastward beyond the Ayton crossroads and Parbroath. In 1791, the *First Statistical Account of Scotland*[12] described the parish as having 'a large bog or morass, one mile long and half a mile broad.' The *Second Statistical Account* (1836) recalled: 'An extensive tract of ground was covered with brushwood…[and] a coarse and rank grass, which afforded a scanty nourishment to the few half-starved cattle that waded about in search of subsistence.'

But (said the *Second Account*) there had been many changes for the better. The great bog had been drained *c.*1800 using clay pipes made in Cupar, and 'What was once a noxious morass is now good and valuable land… converted into fruitful corn-fields.' One settlement beside a especially wet patch had been called Bogtown[13] but after the draining it gained the prettier name of Blinkbonny. The earth was rich but very soft, and traces of the past remained: 'In this mossy soil, there are still found pieces of

---

[9] 'Ballinbreich [castle] stands high/Higham in a hollow/Glenduckie in a swampy drain/and Moonzie on a hill.' Thanks to Michael Struthers and Eric Titterington for this. There are rival versions in some of which Glenduckie stands in a 'waterdub'.

[10] e.g. in Macleod. Taylor thinks 'bog' is in fact the Gaelic *bolg*, or round swelling hill i.e. 'the fort on the round hill', though no fort has been found on Dunbog Hill.

[11] The James Gordon (1642) map, and the Gordon and Joan Bleau (1654) map of 'The Sheriflome of Fyfe' (1654) on the National Library of Scotland website. In 1692 it is referred to as the 'moss of Dunbog'. The water was canalised *c.*1800 into the Fernie Burn.

[12] For simplicity, I shall refer to this and two succeeding studies as the *First, Second and Third Accounts*. Full references are given in the bibliography.

[13] It can be seen with the old name on Ainslie's (1775) map reproduced by Taylor.

oak trees, black as ebony, which must… have lain there for many centuries.' Even today, road repairs sometimes turn up fragments of black oak, and there are patches of old swamp beside the Ayton woods and also between Dunbog Hill and Inchrye, where the drainage system starts.[14]

Communications before 1800 were awkward, and the roads and tracks held to the hills to keep out of the wet. James Ainslie's map of 1775 shows a track running along the sides of Norman's Law and Glenduckie Hill and on to Newburgh, but no road east-west through the low lying centre of Dunbog.[15] The axis of communication was north-south, from Higham on the ridge over the Tay, south through Glenduckie, across the burn and into the incongruously grand avenue of trees to Dunbog, and onwards south again towards Monymail. After the gitterhole was drained, however, in 1802 an east-west road could be opened where the A913 is today, across the lowland in the middle, linking Cupar with Newburgh and passing the future site of the hall.

In 1848, the railways edged closer, the line from Perth to Edinburgh turning south just short of Dunbog, at Glenburnie by Lindores Loch, but the line eastward through Dunbog was not opened until 1909. Meanhile, *Westwood's Directory* (1866) records a long daily walk for the postie:

> A walking postman leaves the [Newburgh] Post Office about 9 a.m… reaching Dunbog at 10.45. He then crosses Glenduckie Hill and walks east to the Manse of Flisk… [returning to] Newburgh before 4 p.m.

Draining away the people

It was not only the water that was drained away. The 19th century historian John Leighton claimed that *c.*1700 there were some 400

---

[14] The field drains at Inchrye can be seen looking down from the slopes of Dunbog hill, and are shown on modern Ordnance Survey maps.
[15] The relevant portion of the map is reproduced in Taylor, or can be seen on the National Library of Scotland website.

Dunbog School, and neighbouring ponies

people in Dunbog parish, but that by 1801 the population was down to 232. Leighton wrote:

> Within the memory of man there was a village near the kirk in which a weekly market was held. The improved system of agriculture which has been introduced, having led to the enlargement of the farms, soon depopulated the village, and it has now entirely disappeared.[16]

By 1836, there were just 170 people; the numbers only rarely touched 200 and the parish records show falls in the farming population over three centuries. That 'improved system' of larger

---

[16] Leighton (1840). This claim is repeated in *Westwood's Directory* for 1862. The 1866 edition of *Westwood's* states simply that Dunbog 'contains no village or hamlet.'

commercial farms also meant enclosure of fields, more drainage and then mechanisation, and as labour needs fell there began the steady drift of people to the towns and overseas, exacerbated by the rapid decline in linen weaving in the cottages. The farms continued the slow business of growing bigger by swallowing each other up, a process that persists today. Most of our proud, four-square farmhouses date from the 19th century period of consolidation, but many of these have now lost their fields: Denmuir, Dunbog, Glenduckie, Higham, and Johnston old farmhouses all have much reduced land. In the parish there are several large stone farm steadings; a few of these do still work as agricultural buildings (e.g. at new Higham), but many are either ruinous or have been converted to housing, such as the 1827 Inchrye Priory steading which stood derelict for years.[17] One substantial farmhouse – Old Higham – appears with a large complex of buildings on the 1855 *Ordnance Survey* map, but was abandoned *c*.1947 in part for lack of water (in Dunbog!) and, after being occupied by a shepherd for a while, fell into ruin.[18]

Meanwhile, as mechanised farms employed ever fewer people, the farm cottages housed fewer families. Some like the Old Higham cottages fell derelict. At neighbouring Kinnaird, the farmer[19] received a letter from Fife Council declaring that his five ruinous cottages were a blot on the landscape and should be pulled down. Other cottages copied the farms and grew by absorbing each other. The Glenduckie house in which I live was at one time three labourer's cottages of two rooms each, but by the 1970s one end was uninhabited, or at best used as a bothy. With no bathroom, a stone floor and walls and no insulation of any sort, it must have been miserable. In the early 1980s it was occupied by goats. The

---

[17] This was renovated in 2021-2 as a group of expensive, energy-efficient homes with heat pumps and triple glazing.

[18] It had already (1909-11) been superseded as the farmhouse by 'new' Higham. The old house has been rebuilt with a decent water supply and solar panels (2013-14). Occupation by shepherds was often the final stage in a house's decline, as at Denmuirhill, now a ruin.

[19] William Craig; his son Gordon still farms there. The derelict cottages were replaced by one house following the outline of the old walls.

building was altered *circa* 1987. Today, two adults live in what was once three family homes.

Inchrye steading before the 2021 renovation into eco-homes.

The reputation of the people

The building of Dunbog Hall had to do with the character of the community. The 1791 *First Statistical Account* said of Dunbog, 'The people are industrious, and there is only one ale-house.' The 1836 *Second Account* continued the good news: 'The climate is mild and salubrious, and no better proof of this can be adduced than the robust health of the inhabitants, and the great old age to which many of them attain.' That great old age could be a problem, then as today, for who would support the very old if they had no family? In 1836 the parish was giving money to thirteen on the poor roll; many were elderly. There were also two families of orphan children, and there might be widows such as Janet Wilkie and her three children who received 6/- weekly. The parish did its best to care for the young, and there has been a school since at least 1672. The *Second Account* reported, 'There is no person in the parish unable to read and write, but many who read and write very ill.'

The people of Dunbog had a name for generosity. The Kirk Session minutes from the 17th century[20] tell of the parish sending money to assist two men in distant Sligo whose houses had burned down, and also a skipper from Burntisland who had been captured by Turks and taken to Algiers. The Rev. Dr Adam Cairns[21] in the 1836 *Second Account* wrote that his parishioners the Dunbog ploughmen were tough, honest and kind.

But, in the eyes of some, the community was not all it should be. Morals, attitudes and social cohesion were doubtful. The problem (thought Dr Cairns) lay in the nature of agricultural labour, in particular the evil of male farm workers living together:

> It is a melancholy truth that this interesting race of our people has been allowed to sink into a state of great ignorance and debasement. One chief cause of this calamity, we do not hesitate to say, is the practice universal in Fife, of making the young unmarried men live together in bothies… In these hovels, the wicked speedily corrupt the good. The old ensnare the young, and the hardened profligate leaves no effort untried to seduce the scrupulous and timid… Until this horrid system be abolished, it will be in vain to expect any happy alteration in the character and condition of our ploughmen.

Other writers believed that community spirit was inevitably lacking in a population that kept moving. The stereotype of rural communities pinned to the land is not wholly true. Stability was in proportion to status and income: the larger landowners and nobility might stay in their houses or castles for generations; the

---

[20] 17th century Session minutes are examined in Buchan.
[21] Dr Cairns married the sister of John Ballingall who farmed Collairnie and Aytoun.

tenant farmers usually had a lease of nineteen years; the labourers shifted annually. At Martinmas (28th November), the end of their working year, Dunbog labourers would go to the hiring fair at Fluthers in Cupar; many would engage themselves to a different farmer, and would move on to a new farm and often to a new district. Dr Cairns in the 1836 *Second Account* again:

> Another grand cause of this flagrant evil is to be found in the fluctuating and wandering lives of the ploughmen themselves. The married men frequently, the unmarried men always, 'flit' at the end of one year's service.[22] They thus acquire vagrant habits and uncontrollable minds. They are never long enough in one place to form useful connections… or to receive any advantage to their children from the care and superintendence of a parochial teacher. They thus virtually cut themselves off from all the blessings of Christianity and civilization, and in a land of light are literally roaming about in darkness.

A Royal Commission of 1893[23] enquired into the condition of Fife's agricultural labourers and came to a similar conclusion in less colourful language, noting a 'restless spirit within the workforce'. The Dunbog School Board minutes for 1915 mention a proposal to create a 'Branch School Bank… as a means of encouraging and promoting thrift on the part of the scholars.' But the Board was doubtful of its success, 'due to the migratory habits of a considerable portion of the population.'

Some of these rootless people also had unsound religious ideas – or so believed John Leighton, writing of Dunbog in 1840. They were 'dissenters' from the Established Kirk, 'but as they are so often removing, it is impossible to speak precisely as to their number.' Ironically one such would be the minister himself, Dr Cairns, who came out for the Free Kirk at the Disruption of 1843 and then flitted to Australia in 1851.

---

[22] According to Macleod, single men sometimes only signed up for six months.
[23] Pringle, R.H. *Reports.*

So Dunbog's better sort – the landowners, professions, educators, and the Kirk – fretted that their hold on the labour, morals, opinions, and savings of the working classes was not as firm as they would have liked. In 1836, Dr Cairns had declared that it was up to 'the masters and clergy to unite in a zealous endeavour to reclaim to better habits the labouring class of our people.'

The Kirk had become increasingly concerned as Scottish congregations began to fall away in the mid-19th century. Enthusiastic movements attempted to re-ignite popular piety, and there was a belief that kirks needed to be larger to make space for disappointed worshippers who supposedly didn't turn up because there was nowhere to sit. Dunbog's 1803 kirk was therefore extended in 1856 although, as there was already seating for 197 people and the entire parish population was only *c.*200, it is difficult to see who else they hoped would come.[24]

Another trend was known as 'practical religion', a feature of which was the building of church halls for community activities of a sound moral character.

The fear of moral instability went back a long way. The 18th and 19th century Kirk Session minutes for Dunbog reveal a determination to impose moral authority on the labouring poor, especially the 'farmservants' (farm labourers). It is not altogether clear what had happened when, in 1860, we read the Dunbog Session summoning –

> George Adamson farmservant at Higham and his spouse Elizabeth Low, also David Mitchell farmservant at Higham and his spouse Mary Ann Stewart who confessed themselves severally guilty of antinuptial fornication.

Notice the spelling: this is 'anti-nuptial' (against marriage), not 'ante-nuptial' (pre-marital). These four people have spouses, they are married already; is this an instance of wife-swapping? The

---

[24] The Kirk Session noted 136 communicants in 1862, with numbers holding up in 1928 when 128 "sat down at the Lord's table" i.e. took communion.

Dunbog Kirk Session minutes are full of sinners 'solemnly rebuked' for fornication. In the 1850s, when statistics were first published, it was realised that illegitimacy rates were higher in Scotland than in most of Europe, and worse in the countryside than the towns. Isabella Wakefield was hauled before Dunbog Kirk Session in May 1862, because she had 'brought forth a child in uncleanness' (illegitimately).

The poor might not take kindly to being rebuked; as time passed they resented the interference more openly, and began to answer back. In 1890 Ann Davidson was called to Dunbog Kirk Session for fornication, but her father said she was ill and could not attend. In 1891 the Session called her again, but when she appeared she protested that, whatever it was she had done, 'she had never got anything, and Ellis was now living in Edinburgh.'

Where the occupation of the sinners is given in the Kirk Session minutes, we see that it was always the poor who got into trouble: 'farm servants', ploughmen and their women. There is no record of any dignitary or gentleman being summoned.

Much of the blame (according to sound opinion) lay with poor education. Both clergy and teachers were badly paid, so much so that – said the 1791 *First Statistical Account* – unless things improved, they would become 'objects of compassion' and 'their weight must be lessened'. Meanwhile, 'the very small encouragement given to schoolmasters is one of the greatest evils.' The salary of teachers was tiny, and 'What man fit to teach can live upon this? A common tradesman can live more at his ease.' The lesson was obvious: 'Imperfect teaching of youth is like bad plowing in spring, which must of necessity produce a bad crop in harvest.'

Morals and education are themes that recur throughout the story of Dunbog Hall.

Doocots caused tension between gentry and tenant farmers, as the birds ate crops. The 1724 double doocot at Denmuir still has its roof today.

1864: The Gunpowder Plot

The celebrated Dunbog Gunpowder Plot of 1864 showed just how unruly the people could be. It made the national news. Rural Fife may be a long way from London, Paris and St Petersburg, but those years saw the international spread of something new and frightening: anarchist terrorism. The proponents of anarchism – Kropotkin, Proudhon and others – had written of the absolute right of the individual to freedom from institutional control. Across Europe from the early 1860s people with agendas were exploding bombs; it was known as 'the propaganda of the deed.'[25]

---

[25] i.e. 'deeds speak louder than words'. After the various failed European revolutions of 1848, individuals and small groups used bombs to attack oppressive regimes. In 1881 they blew up Tsar Alexander II. A congress of anarchists met in London that year. Joseph Conrad's 1907 novel *The Secret Agent* evokes the times nicely.

Gunpowder was the early weapon of choice, then nitroglycerine and dynamite.

In 1862, the minister of Dunbog moved away to another parish, so the congregation began to look for a replacement; in their opinion, it was up to them to choose their preacher. They interviewed ten candidates and elected a man from Anstruther. But when they informed the authorities, they were told that the Crown had chosen someone for them, a Rev. James Edgar from Berwick.

The people of Dunbog were outraged. They sent petitions to the Home Secretary and the Church authorities. They wrote to the press, alleging corruption and nepotism. The authorities stood firm: they decided who would be the minister, not the people.[26] But Mr Edgar began to receive letters:

> 'I write as a friend to let you know if you are still determined to come here… you may expect to meet with something which will cause you much trouble… so come prepared for your fate… I am one of the hard-working classes, and a parishioner of Dunbog.
>
> P.S. Both person and property of an intruder will be exposed to danger here.'

On 10th July 1863, the day Mr Edgar arrived in Dunbog, black flags – of protest, even of anarchy[27] – were flying from Norman's Law, Glenduckie and Dunbog Hills. An effigy of a minister in clerical dress was found hanged in a tree near the school. Just fifteen people came for the inauguration service, all of them strangers save for three local objectors, these standing and demanding to be heard and being threatened with expulsion. No one in the congregation would agree to serve as an elder. Reports

---

[26] The Established Kirk was still nervous after the 1843 Disruption in which clergy and congregations had defied the authority of the Church to appoint ministers.

[27] If these were really understood as *le drapeau noir*, the symbol of anarchism, then Dunbog would have been in the vanguard of fashion. Black flags of protest were seen in Lyon silk workers' strikes in 1831 and demonstrations in Glasgow in 1832, but an association with anarchism is usually said to begin with the Paris Commune of 1871.

went to London; a headline in the *Spectator* magazine read: 'Dunbog in Revolt'.

The former Dunbog manse, modernised in the 1990s.

Then, in October 1864, someone packed gunpowder into the iron bush (hub) of a cartwheel, placed this against a window of the manse, and blew it up. The dining room was wrecked and sharp splinters of metal were found lodged in the ceiling, piercing through to the boards of the room above. Fortunately for Mr Edgar, he was not at home. Meanwhile, obscene, libellous and threatening letters were sent to him through the Dunbog post office. One letter, regretting that the bomb had failed, threatened to blow Mr Edgar's head off if he should step outside the manse. No one was ever arrested for the bomb, but John Bell of Glenduckie was prosecuted for sending the letters and leading the sedition. At his trial in Perth, a young woman stood up: Elizabeth Edmiston was described as 'rather good looking' and living with her father at Ayton smiddy.[28] No, she confessed, it was her had sent the letters 'merely for a frolic'. She was tried at Edinburgh in January 1866 and sentenced to five years hard labour.

Rev. James Edgar

---

[28] Anon., *The Dunbog Case*. John Bell was the tenant at Glenduckie farm, and had raised funds to build the school's clock tower. He had a sad end, becoming mentally unstable. In 1877 he walked in his stockings through the snow over Glenduckie ridge and drowned in the Tay.

Mr Edgar stayed at Dunbog for three decades, until not long before the hall was built.[29] He was remembered as a kind man. But he never got over his first ordeal, and for the rest of his life he suffered from a violent nervous trembling. A photograph shows him in habitual pose with the fingers of his right hand held to his temple, to keep his head steady.

Such was the reputation of the common people of Dunbog: generous and strong, but of dubious sexual and religious leanings, and inclined to take matters into their own hands – and so rootless that it was a fair question, whether they were truly 'the people of Dunbog' at all.

1910-14: Before the building of the Hall

It is sometimes imagined that Britain before World War One lived in a warm post-Edwardian glow. We fondly envisage tight-knit communities for whom work was hard but society was stable, with a hierarchy of gentry, professions and labouring classes. Not an idyll exactly, but culturally rich, steeped in tradition and slow to change. This was the world that the 1914-18 war supposedly blew apart.

Few historians would accept that picture. The authorities before 1914 had many reasons to fear rapid changes in British society, changes that the war in some cases accelerated but often merely delayed by four years. The world prickled with tensions and conflicts, many of them violent. Revolution was brewing; activists had lately killed the Kings of Portugal and of Greece, and the Presidents of both France and the USA. 1913 saw Britain's first national railway strike, during which protesters in Wales fought battles with the police; they were fired upon by the Army, with several deaths. The suffragettes were engaged in a campaign of arson – Leuchars station was burned – and in 1910 the 'Battle of Parliament Square' lasted for six hours with 115 women arrested

---

[29] He was there until 1893. The new Parish Council was formed in 1894, and soon got to work on plans for the hall.

and many injuries. Civil war threatened over Irish Home Rule; 20,000 German rifles and three million rounds of ammunition were intercepted being smuggled in for a loyalist uprising. Huge parades of Ulster Volunteer loyalists – some reports said 100,000 – were held in April 1912, declaring that they would fight to stay loyal to the British Crown.

Would farm labourers in Dunbog have known any of this? Why not? Scottish farms employed gangs of Irish seasonal workers, and many Fife farming families had come from the West Coast and closer contact with Ireland. Irish labour was important in the Dundee mills. Communications were improving, and in 1909 the Newburgh & North Fife Railway opened, passing through the parish. This brought a promise of modernity and all the more news from the outside world (as well as a ready means of loading up your property and leaving).

Meanwhile, the Labour movement was militant. In 1912, 41 million working days had been lost through industrial action; in 1913 there were 1,459 strikes. A 'Triple Alliance' of big unions was formed: miners, dockers, and railwaymen. Joint action by these would have had severe consequences for Dunbog families, affecting food and domestic fuel supply, employment, transport, and the shipping of farm produce. In 1912, Joseph Duncan was appointed by the TUC to establish the Scottish Farm Servants Union – but, ironically, Duncan suffered from that same mobility of the working population that worried the authorities. Farm workers did not stay put long enough for the union to become well established, and the farm labourers never did strike.

But agriculture was in a poor state; Fife farmers were finding it very hard to make a good income, with imports of cheap food undercutting prices. As a consequence, many tenants were abandoning their farms; unoccupied, they fell derelict. While some families (such as the Arbuckles) arrived in Fife from the west coast, there were others who decided to move south to East Anglia where the climate and the soil were easier. Where farmers struggled, farm workers and their families suffered. The authorities were well aware of this; there were several commissions enquiring into the state of agriculture and conditions for working families, and the picture was grim. One study was called *The Tyranny of the Countryside*.[30] A 1913 enquiry by May Kendall and B. Seebohm Rowntree, called *How The Labourer Lives*, began:

> How to stop the steady drift of the population to the towns? That problem... has become so acute that it can no longer be shelved while 'more urgent' matters receive attention.

The loss of population was enormous. Sixty years beforehand (wrote Kendall and Rowntree), half the population of Britain had lived in the country, half in the towns, but by 1913 it was one person in the country to every four in town. This continued, and the inter-war period would see a peak in Scottish emigration: in just ten years, between 1921 and 1931, the population of Flisk dropped by 25%. In tiny Glenduckie village, two cottages fell into ruin and disappeared. Life in country areas was just too hard, and wages too low. Kendall and Rowntree concluded that perhaps a third of British rural families lived in poverty.

The government was certainly worried, and offered support. In 1908 state pensions were introduced. 1911 was the year of the National Insurance Act, providing unemployment benefit, sick pay and health care from 'panel doctors', and in 1913 the first of these became available. But few of the rural poor had as yet seen such benefits, and many felt disconnected from politics. In 1911, a majority of Scottish adults still had no vote. Although Dunbog Parish Council was elected, the franchise required a minimum of twelve months residence at one address, thus excluding most of the population of labourers shifting cottage each Martinmas.

People may have been poor, but that doesn't mean that they were politically ignorant; the press was reporting turmoil in Ireland, Russia, Spain, the Balkans, and elsewhere. Internationally, the working class was getting uppity, and Dunbog had 'history';

---

[30] F.G.Green, 1913.

they might blow up the manse again if they suspected oppression. In the words of the *Second Account*, Dunbog labourers had 'vagrant habits and uncontrollable minds.' Perhaps they whispered sedition in their bothies – who could tell?

Who built Dunbog Hall – and why?

The building of community halls was common throughout the late 19th and early 20th centuries. Many town halls, big and small, are Victorian: Markinch built theirs in 1857, Auchtermuchty in 1865. Village halls generally appeared rather later, and are sometimes associated with the end of the First World War, with appropriate names: the Victory Hall at Collessie, the Memorial Hall at Gateside.

But other halls were built before the outbreak of war. In part this came about through changes in administration. The Local Government (Scotland) Act of 1894 established elected Parish Councils across the country. Dunbog Council was one of these. The new Parish Councils took on various local responsibilities such as administering Poor Law relief, education at primary schools, and supervision of Lunacy orders (and in 1913, Mary, wife of a shepherd at Higham, had to be removed to the District Asylum). But these were matters that had long been managed by the parish kirk sessions anyway, so local control was no great departure.[31] Reading the minutes of the new Parish Council, one can hear the councillors asking: *What else shall we do?* In many places, what they did was build a village hall.

What were the motives? Partly, no doubt, it was an 'improvement' of the sort councils anywhere plan for, a modernisation to go with the new railway. It may have seemed timely and fitting since Dunbog parish had recently become substantially bigger, absorbing in 1891 all of Ayton, Denmuir, and Norman's Law which had previously been a detached offshoot of Abdie parish. No doubt also there was an element of keeping up

---

[31] Responsibility for the poor had been transferred to Poor Law boards in 1845.

with the neighbours – although, in our neighbourhood, several parishes had not got round to it by 1914: Gauldry Hall dates from 1896, Craigrothie from 1907 and Luthrie from 1909, but the little parish of Flisk never has had a hall, while Abdie's dates only from 1925. The oddity of Dunbog is that there was no village. There was a thinly scattered population, but there had not been a village as such for generations.

Then why the need for a hall? Possibly the absence of a village suggested the need for a focal point.[32] But we've seen how the labourers were a cause for concern. This was not new. In the early 19th century, social reformers were calling for 'rational recreation'. This was aimed at the rapidly growing populations of industrial towns who were seen to be sliding into debauch, sedition, and drink. What was needed (it was thought) was temperance, worthy associations, libraries, classes, healthful exercise and other activities to occupy the mind and keep the workers out of pubs.[33]

The 'rational recreation' movement spread out to the country where the problems were different but the perceived wants were similar. In unsettled times, any facility that might encourage labouring people to stay put would seem to be a benefit, anything to encourage loyalty, identity and cohesion. There was a need for organised social gatherings for men and women, for better education, entertainments, and a safe venue for political meetings – anything other than grumbling in the bothies. The people wanted added value in their lives, and the authorities wanted the people gathered under their wing.

Who were 'the authorities' in Dunbog in 1914? Set over the restive lower classes was that grouping of interests often known as the Establishment: landowners, the kirk, the military, the professions, and the politicians, working through a class of

---

[32] In other parts of the country – for example, Aberdeenshire – there are many scattered communities with no village or focus other than a school and a hall. But this is not common in Fife.

[33] Or, at least, in controllable and worthy institutions like the 'Goth' pubs of the mining communities of south Fife, where some of the profits went towards social needs.

Dunbog school and house (1839). Funds for the clock (1857) were gathered by John Bell of Glenduckie, the tenant farmer at Glenduckie accused of sedition in 1863.

managers. In a community so small, the managerial class was even smaller, and often doubled up its roles. In 1866, Mr William Black was Dunbog schoolmaster, sub-postmaster, and also Registrar of Births, Deaths and Marriages. In 1923, Mr James Anderson held the posts of Dunbog schoolmaster, Inspector of the Poor, Clerk to the Parish Council and the Hall Committee, Kirk Session Clerk, and Registrar. In 1952 Miss Edith McPherson was the Dunbog school headteacher, and the Registrar, was also organist at the kirk, and had previously been hall secretary. Everything overlapped: the Parish Council held its meetings in the school, and then at the hall, while the school contained the parish branch library and was for a while a sub-post office too. The same family names re-combined in the armed forces, kirk, and big house: at Dunbog, the son of a General married a minister's daughter, while a daughter of an Admiral married the Dunbog minister.[34]

---

[34] Not happily, however. The Admiral's daughter and the minister were wed in 1903

The kirk was heavily involved in both school and hall. The minister of Dunbog was usually chairman of the hall committee, and the link had a practical advantage: Dunbog Kirk had gained charitable status (for tax purposes) in 1904, with the parish hall recognised as a branch of the kirk. There was also an enduring association with the armed forces, and kirk and military might overlap; during WW1, a young clergyman called J.W.Arthur raised a body in Kenya to assist the struggle: the Kikuyu Missions Volunteer Carrier Corps. He was rewarded with an OBE, and became both minister of Dunbog (1938-48) and hall chairman. His photograph now in Abdie Kirk shows a man of thoughtful demeanour with campaign ribbons on his clerical dress. Rev. McDonald, Dunbog minister from 1955, had been an army chaplain in WW2 with the Highland Light Infantry and the Argylls. A succession of forces officers served on Dunbog Hall committees, including the 1914 founding chairman, Lt Colonel Middleton. He was followed by Captain Simpson in the 1930s; Major Lawson in the 1950s; Major Fullerton-Carnegie, a 1950s trustee; Major Innes, the hall secretary c.2000; then John Gritten from the RAF, and Philip Todd, formerly with the Black Watch.

Dunbog Hall was, however, primarily the result of a deal between the new Parish Council and a major landowner, for the landed nobility also had a clear interest in a stable society. Most farmers in Dunbog were tenants of estates, and could not give away land for a building; the donor of the land in 1914 was one of the great magnates of Scotland. The Dundas family had acquired property in Flisk and Dunbog in the mid-18th century.[35] In 1914 the head of the family was the Most Honourable Lawrence Dundas, Marquis of Zetland,[36] Earl of Ronaldshay, Baron Dundas KT ('Knight of the Thistle'). Sir Lawrence had no ancient connection with Fife; the Dundas fortune had been made by his forebear the

---

but the marriage was annulled in 1904. She soon married again, but he never did. For a man in the public gaze, this must have been difficult to bear.

[35] "Sr Lau Dundas Bart"appears on the 1775 Ainslie map as owner of 'Bambriech'.

[36] The archaic 'Zetland' was used by Shetland County Council until 1975. It is a crude rendering of the Norse spelling. Dundas had no particular link to the islands.

first Sir Lawrence, a businessman from Kerse near Falkirk who sold supplies to the army that crushed the Jacobites, for which he was well rewarded. At much that same time (1762-3), while old Sir Lawrence was purchasing a chunk of Dunbog, he also bought Aske Hall in Yorkshire and moved the family pomp there. They later acquired the title of Zetland for further services, and remained feu superiors of part of Dunbog, including the hall, right up to the abolition of feudal rights in Scotland in 2003.[37]

But whose idea was the hall? Perhaps Colonel William Middleton, the chairman of the new Parish Council? If the idea originated within the Council, they may have come up with it soon after their formation in 1894. These – and not the 'farm servants' – were the people and the interests behind the building of Dunbog Hall.

The Hall is begun

The process was a slow one. Lawrence Dundas, Lord Zetland, had land to spare; he owned sizeable parts of Stirlingshire, Clackmannan and Linlithgow, besides the Flisk estate in Fife which included three Dunbog farms.[38] He clearly approved the notion of a hall. But not even a grandee could give away his land on a whim. Like many large landowners, Zetland properties were held in an 'entail'. This was to stop Dundas frittering away the estate and inheritance in gambling and loose living, ruining the family.[39] He had to seek permission, and that took time.

---

[37] So I am advised. The family sold the Flisk Estate in 1982 to Legal & General Assurance, but most likely opted to retain the feu superiority for simplicity's sake and perhaps for historic reasons, up until the 2003 abolition. The property is confusingly named: 'Flisk Estate' was sometimes used for their Fife holdings, 'Kerse Estates' for all their Scottish lands.

[38] Higham, Dunbog, and Johnston farms.

[39] Some were facing ruin anyway. The big Scottish estates had serious financial difficulties at this time, which would then be exacerbated by severe new inheritance and other taxes imposed in 1918. Something like 20% of Scottish landed property changed hands in the decade after WW1.

The Dunbog avenue of trees is of 18th century origin, and appears on the 1775 John Ainslie map of Fife.

In October 1901, Dundas petitioned the Court of Session in Edinburgh asking to be allowed to offload some land, which would include the plot for Dunbog Hall.[40] Permission was granted in January 1902, with the condition that Dundas asked permission also of his son John (part of whose inheritance he would be giving away, after all).

Ten years later, in 1912, the Zetland estates and the Parish Council were in formal discussions about a hall, and by the spring of 1914 the terms of the gift of land were agreed. Not that Colonel Middleton would have dealt directly with Dundas; they almost certainly never met. The heart of the family's landholding was in

---

[40] The petition to 'dispone' land is set out in detail at the beginning of the hall's feu contract, in order to make it clear that Lord Zetland had permission to make the grant.

Stirlingshire and at their 'seat' in Yorkshire; no Dundas had ever lived for long on the Flisk estate, and His Lordship is not recorded as ever visiting Dunbog. Colonel Middleton dealt with the estate factor, Mr Charles Brown. Entry was granted as of April 1st 1914, although the contract was not actually registered until January 1915.

The 'feu contract' sets out the terms in detail. The land on which Dunbog Hall now stands is carefully described: 'That piece of ground of irregular shape containing one thousand and thirty six square yards or thereby Imperial measure.' The boundaries were, as now, the Newburgh-Cupar road to the south and the Fernie Burn tributary to the north. Measurements were exact: 'on the road side, it extends following the curve one hundred and forty feet three inches.' Lord Zetland retained mineral rights, including 'all stone quarries, coal, limestone, ironstone, mines and minerals,' but declared that 'no pit shall be sunk from the surface', although if the hall collapsed as a result of His Lordship digging for coal underneath, that was too bad. Dunbog Parish Council was to pay Zetland a feu duty of £2 7/6d yearly.

There were conditions. The parish should build their hall within two years, and the estate would view and approve the plans. The parish could only use the land for the purposes agreed and, if the hall fell into disuse, everything would revert to Zetland. In the tradition of the 19th century social reformers and the temperance movement,[41] all alcohol was forbidden at the hall inside or out. Finally, the parish could not use the hall 'for any purpose that may be deemed nauseous, troublesome or dangerous to the neighbourhood'. It was up to the 'superior' (Zetland) to determine what that meant, and his decision 'shall be final.' If Lord Zetland didn't like what was going on in the hall, he could throw them out.[42]

---

[41] Drink had been seen as a major problem in Scotland; in the 1830s, average consumption for all over-15s was a pint of whisky a week. But intake had been declining steadily ever since. 'Temperance' was a largely spent force by 1914.

[42] Such feu contracts imposed varying conditions. The hall at Craigrothie (Fife) was converted from a school in 1907. Their feu contract stipulates a good stone wall or

But for all the stern language of the contract, relations between between the Zetland estate and Dunbog Parish Council seem to have been cordial and cooperative. Colonel Middleton reported to the council on his meetings with Mr Brown the factor. He'd been given to understand that they need not pay the feu duty; it would be waived 'during Lord Zetland's pleasure.' They should get on and build as soon as they liked. The council called a meeting of parishioners to keep them informed, and work was under way by the summer of 1914.

Lord Zetland would give Dunbog Parish Council the land, but he was not paying for the building. The council now had to raise the money; the records say the hall was paid for 'by public subscription'. Who gave exactly what sums we don't know, but the minutes of the Dunbog School Board for 19th December 1913 show them granting permission to 'the Hall committee' to use the school for a dance and a concert to raise funds, while the Ladies Committee was permitted to hold a fund-raising 'work party'. Another dance was held in February, just two months later. Individual farmers and gentlemen would have given generous donations (this occurs throughout the hall's history). The building was fitted out in early 1915. There would have been an enthusiastic opening; Davie Thomson of Glenduckie relates that his father cycled from near Tayport to be at the first dance. For a tiny community dealing with a great lord and raising a fair amount of money, it was a considerable achievement.

---

fence, and that if the building should become unfit for purpose, it must be demolished and replaced with another 'Public Hall and offices of value exceeding £100.' There was no mention of alcohol or of nauseous activities, but if the Trustees should 'fail to implement' the charter, then the feu superior – Lady Gertrude Cochrane – could expel them 'as if these presents had never been granted', just as at Dunbog. (My thanks to Craigrothie's secretary, Nicholas Morris.)

Dunbog School *c.*1895

Two staff, with 48 children (21 boys, 27 girls). As was often the case, the headmaster was a man (Mr James Anderson) but other teachers were women, who were cheaper. There is a marked variation in the standard of the children's clothing, especially among the boys. By the time the hall opened, many would have been ploughmen, and then soldiers in France.

The original Hall building

What did the new hall look like in 1914? We don't have any plans or description, but we do have two old photographs; one is very small, the other unfortunately not clear enough to reproduce here. But from these we can make out much of the basic shape.

Dunbog hall c.1950, and little changed since 1914 – a small detail from a larger photograph. The car at the door probably belonged to the photographer, Rev. W. Buchan.

The building in the old photographs has none of its present flat-roofed extensions and so is rather smaller, little more than a rectangle. It has a plain flat gable at the west end nearest the school, with two tall windows (now gone). In the middle of the pitched roof there is a tall metal vent, which is still there today, and now has an electric extractor fan mounted under it; in 1914 there was no electricity, so the vent would have worked by natural draught. The hall was lit by oil lamps, and would become quite hot: hence the need for a vent. To the east, we can see that (just as it does today) the roof formed a hip – i.e. not reaching a gable, but with the roof ridge dividing some feet short of the end of the building, and sloping down towards the corners. There is a difference, however: at the original 1914 hip (where the ridge divides) there was a chimney stack; the chimney was thus several feet from the end of the building. The accounts from this period show purchases of coal and firewood; somewhere beneath this there was a stove. It might well have been a tall, round, cast-iron stove of the famous *Tortoise* brand (motto: 'Slow but sure'). The photographs also show that the original end roof, beginning at the hip, was set slightly lower than today, not quite meeting the main ridge. This end roof continued well down, giving a larger lean-to area than today. This annex was a forerunner of the present store-rooms, but in 1914 it had its own external door and a window facing the road. The feu contract speaks of building a hall 'with the appropriate offices'. The lean-to possibly contained a store, with a basic kitchen and a toilet. However, the committee minutes *c.*1936 also specify small charges for the use of the 'ante-room'. Such a room would, I think, have been at this end near the heating – or it may have had its own smaller stove; the old chimney has two pots. Water came from a well. The ground is wet, and the well would not have been deep. But the quality of the water was a worry for decades.

The main entrance faced the road and the porch is still there, with the name over the door: DUNBOG PARISH HALL 1914. There were stone steps up to the road level. There was no car park, but then hardly anyone would have come by car. Almost all parishioners would have reached the hall on foot, with perhaps a few families – the better sort, or from more distant farms – possibly arriving in a horse-drawn vehicle.

We shouldn't suppose, however, that no visitor ever came by car. What about Lord Zetland's factor, or officials from Cupar and

Dunbog Hall 2014

As viewed from the south side of the main road: the hall stands a little below road level. The original building stretched from the left end gable to the hipped right end. The original twin chimney was at the right end of the ridge; the visible chimney at the left dates from the 1950s when a boiler was installed in a cellar. There were formerly two tall windows at the left gable end; these were taken out when the kitchen was built and the cellar dug.

The low flat-roofed extension at the right was built as toilets, but later provided storage for chairs and for the After School Club's gear. The sloping roof originally continued further down, with an 'ante-room' and the first small kitchen. The steel roof vent is still there in the middle of the ridge. The long panel on the roof is for solar-heated water. At the left end, the larger extension is the bar and the smaller the kitchen. The door into the play garden stands open at the left. The small gable facing us is the original porch accessed from the main road, but the main entrance main door is now on the far side of the building, opening into the car park.

beyond? Even before the hall was built, road traffic was a worry to the school next door, as it is today. The School Board minuted a request to the Council 'to erect notice boards intimating to drivers of motor cars the proximity of a school and warning them to drive cautiously.' This request was made in September 1912.[43] Almost from the outset, the building would want improvements and extensions. But they came much later.

Putting the new Hall to use

Colonel Middleton and his Parish Council lost no time. To begin with, a caretaker or 'hall keeper' was appointed. He was Mr James Williamson, and he was to be paid £4 per annum and 2/6d for each evening he was in attendance. His duties were carefully spelled out: lighting the lamps and the heating stove for evening functions; dusting down the chairs and forms (benches); locking up safely at night; cutting the grass, and general maintenance. He was also to ensure that 'no person in a state of intoxication shall be admitted' to any function.

A scale of charges for such functions was also drawn up, and these tell us something of how the hall was supposed to be used:

> Entertainment by non-parishioners – 12/6d
> Private entertainment by parishioners – 5/-
> Social gathering of parishioners – 5/-
> Lectures, readings etc. – 5/-
> Political meetings – 10/-

Notice the charge for political meetings: in an age without radio or television, the public meeting was important for politicians or officials communicating with the populace. The fledgling unions – the new NFU, and the Farm Servants Union – may have been among the political users. The farmers had grave matters to

---

[43] It has remained a worry ever since. See for instance the discussion in the 1977 Community Council minutes (p.83). In 2023 a Fife Council schools manager told me of the grief the Dunbog issue continually gave her.

discuss, above all the economy and prices. The labourers meanwhile were agitating for improved wages. They would have minded their language at Dunbog Hall, for they ran the risk of being thought 'nauseous, troublesome and dangerous.' But it was safer to have them meet where they could be seen.

Early users of the hall included the Women's Guild; the Guild was a branch of Dunbog Kirk, much concerned with charitable works. In a parish like Dunbog – with no village centre, no shops or other meeting place, few opportunities for travel even as far as Cupar, and with no telephones for a blether – the hall would have been a considerable part of social life. For men also: at some point in the early years, a Ploughman's Club was formed.

Even as hall building proceeded, the school was viewing it as an annex; from first opening to the present day, the school has been the hall's principal client. The first idea was for cookery classes. We tend to assume that country families brought up their daughters to be able to cook, but the well-meaning middle-classes of the 19th century thought otherwise, and had lobbied for cookery to be part of the curriculum; 'domestic science' was introduced nationally in 1897. R.H.Pringle's Royal Commission enquiring into the state of agricultural labour in 1893 had noted one of the consequences of farm workers regularly moving farm (and house) with each November hiring fair: a labouring family could give little attention to developing their own garden beyond the basics, while the previous departing family might have left the plot in a sad state. A large part of farm pay was made in potatoes (possibly one ton per family per year),[44] and there was some poultry, pigs and perhaps salt fish, but with little variety, and limited vegetables. In September 1910, it was noted by the Dunbog School Board that the diet of farm-working families was poor;[45] the Board wanted to take action – but had no suitable venue.

---

[44] A 'couped [heaped] cartload per term, or as much as required.' (Macleod)
[45] A limited diet is not necessarily poor nutrition. Several enquiries from the 1860s onward found Scottish agricultural families to be strong and well-nourished – more so than workers in the towns.

In June 1914, however, the School Board minutes mention that the parish hall now 'in course of erection' would be the place, if given a satisfactory water supply. In 1915, Fife Council Education Committee approved the school asking to use Dunbog Hall for 'giving instruction in cookery.' This was agreed, for a charge to the school of 2/6d a time, once a suitable teacher could be found. A year later the arrangement was expanded to include 'buttermaking and dairying' classes for girls over 12 years of age. Again, one might have thought that country families would have known what to do with milk, but Dunbog was not a dairy parish.[46]

Meanwhile, the School Board was deciding which days they would run up the Union Jack. It would be the King's Birthday (June 3rd), Empire Day (24th May), Waterloo Day (18th June) and Trafalgar Day (21st October). This was solid bellicose patriotism – and about to become all too real.

1914-18: The Great War in Dunbog

Even as Dunbog Hall was built, the world took a turn for the worse. An entry in the early Parish Council minutes gives a sideways glimpse of the impact of the war: in April 1915, with the building not long finished, Mr Adamson of Kingskettle applied to hold regular dancing classes in the new hall. His request was put on hold: 'It was agreed to ask the applicant to postpone his application in view of the state of national affairs.' Dancing would have been unseemly.

Out of a total parish population of *c*.200, thirty-eight Dunbog men went to war. This must have been most of the able-bodied. The newly opened Newburgh & North Fife Railway passing through the parish closed briefly for lack of workforce. Proportionate to population, Scotland lost a high percentage of its

---

[46] Buchan (*Parish of Dunbog*) does however note in the 18th century Kirk Session records the parish giving money to help certain 'cottars' to buy a cow, and it was common for a supply of milk to be one of the perks of a farm labouring job. (Macleod).

men in WW1 (as is vividly conveyed in Grassic Gibbon's *Sunset Song*). A majority of those from Dunbog served in France with the Black Watch or the Argylls, although Bombardier Paton Tocher found his way to Calcutta with the Cassipore Artillery. Farm boys were considered excellent recruits – strong, used to hard work, and disciplined – but it was the officers who got Dunbog's decorations: two Military Crosses, one Military Medal. The effect on the community was felt in many ways, not least the requisitioning of horses.

At Denmuir, just below Norman's Law, a rifle range was built. This can be seen on the 1920 OS six-inch map, and the target machinery is still there today: six very rusty pulley mechanisms for lifting cloth bullseye targets above a high stone wall and protective earth bank. The firing positions were at increasing distances backing onto Whirly Kips hill, and the targets had Norman's Law as a solid backdrop, although the gunfire must have been disconcerting for the inhabitants of Denmuirhill cottage close by.[47]

In Flanders, mortality among junior officers was usually higher than in the ranks. The Fullerton-Carnegies of Ayton were greatly blessed that their two sons, both lieutenants in the Black Watch, returned alive; George, the elder, brought back two wounds and a Military Cross.[48] The chair of the Parish Council, Colonel Middleton, was an officer (most likely a reservist) in the Scots Greys. His son Archie was a soldier too, and in May 1915 the Middletons received the news every family dreaded, in a letter from Archie's commanding officer with a unit in France:

> Your son was in command of the Grenadiers who attacked the farm (St Julien), and it was near this farm that Archie fell gallantly leading his men.[49]

---

[47] Denmuirhill Rifle Range was still functioning up to 1945, used by recruits such as the Home Guard from Newburgh and Cupar drill halls.
[48] George's own son, Major George Fullerton-Carnegie, was appointed as a hall trustee in 1954.
[49] Archie – A.W.A.Middleton – was educated at Eton and Sandhurst. He had served for some years in India before going to France. He was promoted to Captain in October

The Colonel was not a man to give way to despair, but in July 1918 he resigned from the Parish Council and the hall committee, 'as there was no immediate prospect of his relief from military duties' – although in fact the war had only four months to run. His place as hall chairman was taken by Rev. Middleton Tocher, minister of Dunbog.

Glenduckie farm, 2014. The bays were for machinery, wagons, and horses.

The war was rather good for the economy, with Scottish industry in overdrive producing munitions. The German submarine fleet was causing disruption to those cheap food imports, so Dunbog's farmers had a brief spell of prosperity. The Parish Council followed national directives to ensure that any available waste ground was used for food production, and in September 1917 they established a 'local Food Control Sub-Committee'. This may have met in Dunbog Hall – or in the warmer and more comfortable

---
1914, and was killed on 25th April 1915.

homes of committee members.

The First World War makes only these fleeting appearances in the records of the hall or parish. The one mention in the Kirk Session minutes comes in 1919, recording the installation of a stained glass window paid for by public subscription. The window depicted 'the Christian soldier' and commemorated Dunbog's loss: eleven dead out of thirty-eight.[50] The Colonel himself having survived, the Middleton family offered an illuminated Roll of Honour to be put up in the hall.[51] Even these sad rolls show how transitory was the working population. The memorial for Glenduckie and Flisk was installed on the wall of the old Flisk school but among the names there was not a single family still living in the parish a generation later.[52]

The first property I ever occupied in Scotland (in the mid-1980s) was a converted bothy in Aberdeenshire. As we were planning the roof insulation, I saw something pencilled onto the wooden sarking boards: five men's names, and a year: 1916. With conscription in force, I imagine that those farm boys decided to record their names because they had just been called up for the Army. If they'd got a move on, they would have been in time for the Battle of the Somme.

1918-30: Uneasy with the peace

After the Armistice, the Rev. Tocher continued to chair the hall committee, and Dunbog life returned to normal as best it could, minus eleven young men. In December 1919, Mr Adamson of Kingskettle was allowed to start his dancing classes in the hall, at a charge of 7/6d a night. The Women's Rural Institute asked to use the hall for the first time, and this was agreed for a trial period

---

[50] At 29% mortality, this is roughly double the average for the British services. Others would have been wounded, and may have died of the consequences later. The Fullerton-Carnegie boys, for instance, both died at the fairly young age of 43, one in 1937 and one in 1942.
[51] Both the window and the Roll of Honour are now in Abdie Kirk.
[52] According to the *Third Statistical Account*, 1952.

Reverend Middleton Tocher

of one year at a charge of 4/- per session. (There had been no trial period for the dancing classes.)

In 1922, the minutes record a hope that the hall might buy a piano, although it was not until May the following year that they collected the considerable sum of £47 10/- to purchase one. Charges for its use were agreed: 5/- for a parishioners' concert, 7/6d for a dance, but rather more for use by outsiders. If the WRI wanted to play, that would be an extra shilling. (In December 1928, the hall would lend the piano for a dance at Aytounhill House, for a charge of 10/-.)

And now the general scale of charges for hall use was revised. Non-parishioners would pay £1 for an evening, parishioners only 12/6d. The Ploughmen's Club was to be charged 2/- a session, which was half the rate for the WRI. Another permutation, the Village Club, was charged 4/- nightly.[53] All this evening activity meant income for the new caretaker appointed in 1922, Miss A. Brown. In 1925 she was succeeded by a Mr Charles Currie – the first appearance in the minutes of a family name important in the hall's story.

The Parish Council still had its wider duties, besides running the hall. In 1925 it accepted responsibility for the upkeep of the Dunbog graveyard. Other matters were brought to the council's attention in 1927. Should the local posties be granted a half-day holiday each Saturday?[54] This was the thin end of a wedge; the council 'felt that to allow letters to lie in the local collecting box from 1 p.m. on Saturday to 1 p.m. on the following Monday would be a hardship to the parish.' A more disturbing note also appears: in December that same year the council turned down an invitation to subscribe to the Scottish Society for the Prevention of Cruelty to Children, on the grounds that individual members already donated individually. It was then reported, however, that 'a child

---

[53] This 'village club' only appears once in the hall minutes, but a 'club' was discussed in 2003 after the extensive renovations were completed.

[54] The Saturday half day had been the norm for many Scottish workers – such as the Fife miners – since the 1870s.

was being kept for hire or reward by Mrs Stewart, Higham.'[55] The issue could not be ducked; the chairman and the clerk of the Parish Council were instructed to visit Mrs Stewart 'to see that the conditions of the Children Act of 1908 were being adhered to.'

Mundane concerns continued. The water pump needed mended. They debated buying a fire extinguisher, considered various models, didn't like the type installed at Ayton, and finally got round to purchasing one the following year. In 1926 they installed a curtained 'platform' or stage, larger than we have today.[56] In 1929 the Parish Council sends 'thanks to the Ladies Committee for their kindness in erecting three Aladdin lamps in the hall.'

But of a sudden there came a major upset and uncertainty. New legislation, the Local Government Act of 1929, meant that the political structure of Scotland – a framework which had only been in existence for thirty-five years – was to be altered again. The Parish Council was to be abolished. Local government was to be much less local, and now the school, the poor, the insane, and Dunbog Hall would all be managed by the new District Council at Cupar.

It did not come about instantly. On May 15th 1930, Dunbog Parish Council requested its chairman, Rev. Tocher, to make enquiries at the first meeting of the new Cupar District Council. Nobody quite knew what was going to happen.

1930: Out of control

Control of Dunbog Hall – in particular financial control – together with all other functions of the Parish Council, now passed out of the parish and away to the District Council offices in Cupar, six miles distant. There was still a committee to run the hall, but it was subservient; the new minute book for the hall committee is headed:

---

[55] This presumably refers to some sort of fostering arrangement.
[56] Michael Struthers remembers the old stage as rising some three feet, with steps at the side. Its position can be seen from marks on the present-day floor.

Fife County Council – Cupar District Council
Dunbog Hall local sub-committee

In this, the humble position of the locals in the new structure is apparent. Dunbog people may have considered that it was their hall, their property. They'd had the idea locally, raised the money locally, and had run all the hall's affairs locally, while the same local people were still doing the donkey work. They and their neighbours had done the deal with Lord Zetland. But all that was disregarded; the Parish Council had been absorbed into the District Council, and the hall went with it. This must have rankled.

There is a gap in the available minutes of some five years, between the demise of the old Parish Council in 1929/30 and the new minute book commencing in March 1936. In that interval, systems and procedures for the revised government were being established. But at Dunbog the Rev. Tocher was still chair of the local committee, and we see other names familiar in the parish appearing as committee members in 1936, such as Stirrat and Arbuckle. The hall caretaker was still Charles Currie, whose son Dennis would be a key figure for several decades. At that March 1936 meeting, Charles Currie was applying for an increase in his salary, which was now paid by the District Council.

Meanwhile, the economic depression of the 1930s affected Dunbog in many ways, some of them quite startling.

Bert Spence was an entrepreneurial livestock dealer. He also ran a slaughtering business in Newburgh adjacent to the railway station, and he found himself with a logistical problem: the slaughtering created large quantities of offal that had to be disposed of somewhere. To begin with, it was all taken by cart to fields west of Abernethy, and spread out to rot away. But with time, the land began to suffer from such over-intense 'feeding', so Bert Spence looked elsewhere. Dunbog farm was without a tenant at all; in those dire times, the Zetland estate could find no one to take it on. The land lay fallow. Bert Spence acquired the tenancy for a minimal rent, and at first used the hillside for little more than spreading offal. The guts were brought up from Newburgh by train to a siding at Lindores, and from there carted out and tipped down the slopes of Dunbog hill, to rot.

In the 1920s and 30s, sheep prices were supported by the government in an effort to stop the industry collapsing, and Bert Spence made the most of it. He kept his Dunbog land in grass and bought lambs in the sales early in the year, bringing these also by rail and walking the flock to Dunbog farm. The lambs would be fattened on his grass and then on locally produced turnips, earning the subsidies before being sold on. By some estimates, Bert Spence processed through Dunbog more than forty thousand lambs each season.[57] If nothing else, the noise must have been impressive.

But for many farmers and farming communities, the 1930s were a desperate period. There were many bankruptcies, and worse. Andrew Arbuckle wrote of Fife:

> It was said at the time that no farmer could look out over his neighbourhood without seeing at least one farm where the farmer had either taken his own life or had simply vanished from the scene.

Dunbog Hall was as vulnerable to Depression as the rest of the community; throughout the 1930s there was a slow drip of money worries for the local committee. Cupar District Council kept tight control of the cash, and the hall committee wrote to the Council asking if income from hall letting might now be kept in a 'Hall Improvement Fund' instead of being returned to Cupar. But the Council was unsympathetic. They continued to take the proceeds. In October 1937, however, practical difficulties appeared in this arrangement. Cupar Council had charged the hall £6 9/7d. for 'general expenses' but no one in Dunbog knew what this meant. There was also a deficit in the hall accounts of £28 12/7d, and in Cupar questions were being asked. Rather hurt, the

---

[57] This extraordinary figure was given me by a retired Dunbog farmer, and confirmed as quite likely by a former estate factor.

hall committee pointed out that it was the heating that was costing money, and (say the minutes), 'every effort is being made to make ends meet without calling on the District Rate.'

Kinnaird farm, 1930s: specialist tools but no mechanisation. At harvest, the tatties had to be sorted for size and quality. One man lifts them with a large rake onto riddles of different grades. A man and woman sort them, while to the right another man ties the bags.

In November 1938, the accounts are again showing 'a slight deficiency'. A trend was beginning: the income from use of the hall could not meet the running costs. They had already looked for solutions. In 1936 another revised scale of charges had been introduced:

> Whist drive and dance – £1 for parishioners
> Use of hall to midnight – 12/6d for parishioners
> Non-parishioners £1
> Political meetings – £1
> Ante-room – 2/-

It would be most interesting to know what those 1930s political meetings actually were, but there is no record. There is strong whiff of Depression austerity at this period. The committee wanted to build a store outside to accommodate the chairs and benches, and in November 1936 they considered a corrugated iron shed, but this was considered 'too pretentious'. Possibly (it was suggested) an open-sided timber shelter would do as well? It was also thought that the simple coal stove was insufficient heating, and the committee wanted to install something more modern, but Cupar Council would not pay for it; the hall must raise its own funds. So we see them making plans and organising: there was to be a concert, and a 'dramatic raffle' (curious notion), and also two 'dramatic entertainments', together with the usual whist drives and a dance. It appears that the new heating – coke burning, with radiators – was in place that winter, and was devouring costly fuel.

The best way to keep heating costs down was not to light the boiler. Regular use of the hall by the school was now formalised with an annual fee from the District Council – just £4. Why so little? Because one need not waste money on energetic children: the hall record says, 'Neither heating nor lighting was likely to be required.'

There was little cash available for new facilities. Other users of the hall would have to fund their own needs. In March 1939, the WRI and the Men's Club started raising money to buy a set of card tables for their whist evenings, but it took them nearly a year to find the cash. The folding wooden tables with green baize tops are still in the hall today.

Discarded farm machinery (a grass seeder) in a dark corner, 2014.

Meanwhile, expenditure continued to rise and income to stagnate. As Charles Dickens's character Mr Micawber famously noted: if your annual income is £20 and your outgoings are only £19 19/6d, you are happy. But if your income is £20 and your expenses £20 0/6d, you sink into despair. We see a touch of Micawberism developing in Dunbog Hall committee minutes at this time, with figures remarkably close to those in *David Copperfield*:

> 'The financial statement for the year ended 15th May 1939 was submitted. Receipts amounted to £19 9/6d while expenditure was £20 0/5d, leaving a debit balance.'

The problems were real enough; by November 1940 the operating deficit was £14 and a worry. The committee could only just afford to pay regular bills, and not for improvements or even maintenance. Running repairs were being skimped. In November 1942, the WRI asked for a rebate on the charge for their regular meetings because there were now only two working oil lamps in the hall and they were having to bring their own.

Haymaking with a 'Tumbling Tam' rake. Kinnaird farm, 1930s.

World War Two and other distractions

World War Two impacted physically on Dunbog: three aircraft, perhaps from the training base at Errol, are said to have made forced landings in the parish, one in flames.[58] War also brought an unexpected use for Dunbog Hall: kirk services. In February 1940, Dunbog Kirk asked permission to hold its Easter service in the hall. That same November, the hall minutes again record the

---

[58] I was told this by a Dunbog resident, but have not seen any corroboration.

minister asking to hold services there. No reason is given, but the hall minutes suggest an answer. In the accounts submitted in November 1940, it is noted that there have been some unusual expenses, in particular a new set of blackout curtains; the hall could not have been used for evening functions without these, and that would have effectively have ended its life, so the money was spent. To fit blackout curtains to the big kirk windows, however, would have been enormously expensive – so, as a temporary wartime measure, why not hold evening services in the now blacked-out parish hall?

The people of Dunbog had often responded to distant humanitarian calls on their charity. That did not change. The Kirk Session minutes record that in 1938 a letter was received asking for help on behalf of Czechoslovakian refugees – and the parish responded.[59]

But maintaining community interest in the hall was difficult. In November 1938 the committee resolved on regular twice yearly meetings, so as not to tax the members' enthusiasm. But by November 1942 they were noting that attendance at hall meetings was falling. Quite apart from military service, people were generally more mobile, having more transport available – private cars, public buses, and the train – such that a trip to Perth or Dundee was becoming commonplace, whereas as generation before even an outing to Cupar had been a venture. Perhaps in the context of another world war, a small parish in Fife seemed unimportant.

Perhaps the very idea of a community centre was in trouble. The population was not much more rooted than before; of Glenduckie and Flisk it was stated in 1952 that, 'Almost every house is occupied by farmers or farm workers, and as the tenancy

---

[59] It no doubt helped that the minister (and hall chairman) of Dunbog at this time, Rev. Arthur, had broad horizons. He had been for many years a leading missionary in Kenya, known for representing the interests of the Kikuyu people. But he had got into trouble with the Kikuyu for demanding that all Christians should oppose female circumcision.

of every farm has changed in the last twenty years, it would be hard to find more than half a dozen people who have lived here for more than two generations.'[60] And other strangers had moved in: at Abdie next door, in 1947, 10% of the farm workforce were German PoWs. There had been some change, however. In 1939, the last of the Martinmas 'feeing markets' for farm workers had been held in Cupar. For the duration of the war, in an attempt to reduce inefficiencies in a shifting labour force at a time when so many young men were being called up to fight, a 'Standstill Order' had been in place; farmworkers could only move away with the agreement of the farmer, or by appeal to a tribunal. After the war, the habit of flitting was much reduced. Davie Thomson had a certificate from the Royal Highland and Agricultural Society of Scotland (RHASS) recording thirty years of service on Glenduckie farm, and another certificate for his brother's forty-six years of work for the Craigs of Kinnaird.

But the population of Dunbog remained tiny, still barely two hundred, and shrinking again. The decline can be seen vividly in the numbers on the school roll. The location of Dunbog's first school (mentioned *c.*1660) is uncertain, although on the 1855 Ordnance Survey map the cottage now called 'Briarlea' in Glenduckie is marked as a 'school' – in which case, it must have been very small.[61] By a quirk of boundaries, however, most of Glenduckie is not actually in the parish of Dunbog, but in Flisk, and the authorities might not have wanted a parish school in the wrong parish.[62] Today's site before 1800 was in the marsh. It is possible that another school was at the now-disappeared village at Dunbog itself, near the former mansion and the old kirk.

The current school by the main road dates from 1839, and the

---

[60] *Third Statistical Account.*
[61] This was the 'Female Industrial School' mentioned above.
[62] *Westwood's Directory* (1862) states that, although technically in Flisk, the inconvenience of getting to Flisk church was too great, and so Glenduckie 'was united *quod sacra* [for church purposes] to Dunbog.' The same may have applied to the school. In the *Directory* for 1866, the Glenduckie Female Industrial School is not mentioned, only Dunbog School.

Ordnance Survey Gazetteer of 1882 claims that there was an average attendance of 76 children, with capacity for 120. They must have sat very close together. In the 20th century School Log, the numbers of children keep slowly falling:

1924 – 52	1938 – 35	1960 – 30
1932 – 46	1958 – 33	1965 – 25 [63]

Glenduckie. Where the young trees now stand was once a cluster of cottages which appear on the 1855 OS map but were later deserted.

At the end of WW2, the thirty-odd children were none too healthy; the School Log records outbreaks of scabies, jaundice,

---

[63] When my son started at the school in 2007 the roll was just 23. In 2013 the school had 53 children. This growth is in part because other nearby schools have closed, and in part because Dunbog has a strong reputation, so that children from other areas travel to attend. Dunbog had already absorbed children from Moonzie when their school closed c.1970. In 2014-15 the roll was be nearer 70, a figure not seen since the 1880s. In 2023-4 it is back at 45.

whooping cough, measles and chickenpox. If they were better nourished, that was in part due to the authorities; the 1952 *Third Account* reported that 'School meals and the daily provision of milk have transformed the life of the children, and it is true to say that no reform introduced in the last fifty years has done so much for their physical well-being.' Already, school food was centralised; in March 1947, with roads blocked by severe weather, the Dunbog children were sent home 'owing to the non-arrival of the meal service van from Cupar' – which is not unknown today.

Women's shadows

The decline in the school roll was only one symptom of Dunbog's shrinking population. Another was the disappearance of the women.

In 19th century rural Scotland, the very existence of women was sometimes overlooked. In 1862, the Dunbog Kirk Session noted that they had sixty-four communicants – male communicants, that is. Only as an afterthought did they reconsider, deciding that it might be 'advisable' to count the women as well, and discovering to their pleasant surprise that the total was now one hundred and thirty-six.

The lives of working women were at least as hard as those of the men, and for a long time the women were generally paid only half the wages. The hardest lot was that of the 'in-and-out' girls who by day worked in the fields and, come evening, were expected to cook and clean at the farmhouse.

By the end of the century, things were changing. The 1893 Royal Commission spoke of that 'restless spirit' among the workforce. The investigator, R. H. Pringle, remarked that, 'in many cases it is alleged that the wife is to blame.' Women were getting ideas above their station, and wanting to move on and up. Work in factories paid better and was drier, and town houses while crowded and infested with vermin were at least less wind-blasted.

Dunbog School

Pringle wrote:

> Forty years ago, women working on farms had to take what they could get or go idle, for other employment was scarce and factory life was in its infancy. Now the scene is changed, and no educated girl with a spark of ambition and pride about her need toil among the 'tatties' for lack of opportunities to better herself.

Kendall and Rowntree, in *How the Labourer Lives* (1913), noticed the same restlessness around the country:

> The girls… leave home… Innumerable girls go into service in towns when they are too young and inexperienced to look after themselves… But not all parents can afford to hold on till a suitable situation is forthcoming… 'There isn't a girl in the village beside me,' said one bright young woman of eighteen, who was keeping house for her brother and grandfather, her mother being dead. 'They've all gone away somewhere – into service mostly.'… Field work is no longer an industry that can support a girl at home.

The 1952 *Third Account* said of Glenduckie and Flisk:

> Another feature of the population structure is the preponderance of males. The only kind of work available for girls leaving school is on the land, and, since that no longer appeals so widely, they tend to leave home to work and live elsewhere. On the other hand, it is almost automatic for the sons of the farm labourers to begin work on the farm at 14.

It might have helped if women's labour had received more recognition. In 1914 the RHASS[64] began issuing their medals honouring long farm service, a minimum of 30 years work for one farm or farmer. Women were eligible, but the criteria were (and still are) tight: 'The award is strictly confined to farm workers, such as Ploughmen, Cattlemen, and Shepherds'; others, such as carters or workers in estate forests, did not qualify. Nor did mere farm wives. It is a reasonable assumption that most adult male farmworkers would marry, and their wives both ran the home and – as seen in the 1939 Denmuir tattie planting photograph (*opposite*) – did plenty of the farm work. But in any given year less than 10% of those recognised by the RHASS for their long labouring lives were women. In 1955, for example, 143 Scottish farmworkers received the RHASS medal; only thirteen were women. None of the named women ever 'served' in Dunbog. The records reveal other interest, such as the fondness in farm-labouring families for calling their daughters Wilhelmina, Isabella, and Euphemia.

In the history of Dunbog Hall, the parish women have a shadowy presence. There was a woman as caretaker for three years from 1922-5, and another in 1946. On the hall committee itself, the first woman was Edith McPherson, also school headmistress, who was unanimously confirmed as secretary in December 1936 (she held the post for ten years). But serious negotiations remained men's business; when in 1946 a delegation

---

[64] Royal Highland and Agricultural Society of Scotland, based at Ingliston (Edinburgh). My thanks to them for sharing their records.

was sent to the District Council in Cupar to discuss a revised hall constitution, the delegates were specified as 'three male members of the committee'. Throughout the first 100 years of the hall, there have been a number of women committee members including several secretaries, and currently a woman treasurer, but only in 2023 was the first woman chairperson chosen.

Farmers Weekly, March 24th 1939. Davie Thompson's mother in centre.

"An early start has been made with potato planting at Denmuir Farm, Fife."

Women's activities complemented the men's. The WRI can be glimpsed raising funds and donating lamps, while the Women's Guild (attached to the kirk) helped out with functions. But dancing might have been beyond some housekeeping budgets. Kendall and Rowntree had reported in 1913:

> One labourer's wife, who was comparatively well off as she had a husband and sons working, said that for three or four of them to go to a 'public concert' which had been got up by some local magnate and was to be held in the schoolroom, was quite impossible, as the tickets were 6d each. [Such prices] point to a lack of realisation, even on the part of those who are sincerely anxious to provide some recreation for the people, of the extreme slenderness of their resources.

The Dunbog women still enjoyed their own hall evenings; in 1936 the WRI is recorded as paying 4/6d for hall hire, while the Men's Club at the time was only paying 3/6d. The women, however, had the use of the piano. Perhaps ploughmen didn't play the piano.

Late in the day, it was realised that women's contribution to the parish was crucial. In fact, the hall committee's hand was forced; in 1953 they applied to the Scottish Council for Social Service for a grant under 'the Physical Training and Recreation Act', but they were turned down, apparently because they were unrepresentative and women had no voice; the committee hurriedly appointed the WRI as ex-officio trustees.

It was too late. In the 1952 *Third Account*, Dunbog's WRI is described as 'large and flourishing' and as 'a most useful element in the community'. But something must have soured in the next few years; in 1960 the hall minutes state that there would be no more income from the ladies' musical evenings, because 'the WRI was now finished'.

Crackles on the line

There is a problem shared by all Scottish rural communities: the more sophisticated the expectations of the people, the more services they demand – but services cost money, and a small community cannot generate sufficient income. The population of

A farmworking family, 1960s: Mr and Mrs Thomson at Collairnie farm cottages with their six sons. All but one worked on the land, including Mrs Thomson (seen planting tatties on p.56). "My parents" said Davie (far left), "insisted that we dress properly for tea every Sunday."

Dunbog (and all north Fife) has endured a constant struggle to maintain services. The railway was a symptomatic casualty.

The line from Perth through Newburgh and south towards Edinburgh had been built in 1848, but only in 1909 was an east-west line opened to provide a service along the south side of the

Tay between Dundee and Perth. This was intended to rival the line on the north shore of the river, and to provide passenger and freight services to farms and communities in the north of Fife. The new line passed through the heart of the parish, with the nearest station to Dunbog a mile down the road at Lindores; the Station House is still there, and the old cuttings, embankments and bridges are very evident. There was little romance about it; pre-WW1 railway workers' hours were some of the worst in any industry, and the accident rate rivalled that of the mines.

Railway bridge piers on the Johnston farm lane opposite the hall.

In the early 20th century, the railway was a useful service for farmers and traders, such as Bert Spence bringing wagon-loads of slaughterhouse offal and huge flocks of sheep to Dunbog. Andrew Arbuckle describes how a farm tenant might move his entire stock and gear to new premises by train. Well after WW2, produce from the farms was collected by rail, and this was also the most economical and convenient means for bringing in bulk fertiliser.

But with thirty-one bridges the short Newburgh and North Fife Railway had been expensive to build, and was plagued by problems. One engine managed to fall over at Lindores station. The line was never profitable. There were only at best four services daily in each direction, and those carried fewer and fewer passengers. Journey time between Perth and Dundee was slower than on the north side of the Tay. In May 1923 the NNFR directors were already asking Dunbog Parish Council for support in obtaining a reduction of the rates they paid on land used by the line. Operations were merged with those of North British Railways, but now the NNFR stockholders complained that North British were doing nothing to promote the line, and that it was steadily losing money. When in 1933 a bus company applied to open a service along the same route, this was refused as it might jeopardise the already shaky finances of the railway.[65] The Provost of Dundee was reported as saying that most people had never heard of the Newburgh and North Fife. Inevitably, in 1951 the line was closed to human passengers. It continued to carry potatoes (with *c.*4,000 tons collected from one harvest at Luthrie) but that was not enough, although a few excursion trains passed through.

In 1964 the line closed for good, with a few sad years as an elongated shunting yard for disused rolling stock. Soon the steel track was taken up, and the farmers started laboriously to remove the massive earth embankment that cut across their fields; one was told that he was quarrying without a license, and was to stop selling the rocks immediately. Not everyone wanted the embankment gone; at a public meeting, some Dunbog residents argued that it gave their houses privacy, while others wanted it preserved for wildlife.[66]

---

[65] I am reminded of *The Titfield Thunderbolt*, the Ealing Studios comedy concerning a rivalry between a rural branch line and a bus company. In the film, the train wins; in reality that was unlikely. The film was released, as it happens, in 1952, a year after the NNFR closed to passengers. It includes a dramatic de-railing just as at Lindores.

[66] Both these notions are borne out today by the wooded sections of embankment that remain, for instance between Balmeadie and the main road.

The 'Scottish Rambler' excurson train at Lindores, 1962.

It did not need Dr Beeching to see that the population numbers and the demand had never been sufficient. The Newburgh and North Fife Railway was not alone in these troubles: Fife has 60 disused railway stations, some of them serving private estates, others linked to the declining fishing, flax and coal industries. All across Scotland, railway rolling stock was being sold off for sheds and chicken coops, and by Glenduckie farm for many years there sat an old insulated hot tar wagon, bought for use as a slurry tank. It was finally declared unsightly and removed in 2020.

The hot tar wagon at Glenduckie.

1945-52: Taking the Hall back for the parish

At the end of WW2, it was clear that Dunbog Hall was the worse for wear – and, to the exasperation of the locals, getting Cupar District Council to deal with the problem seemed impossible. There had been frost damage in the hard winter of 1940 but no repairs were done. In 1946, the hall committee joined other locals in petitioning the District Council to bring electricity to the parish, but nothing happened; requests for action seemed to get nowhere. Also in 1946, concerns were raised about the water in the hall well, which they asked the Council to analyse. They were still asking in 1951.

When the 'three male members' of the committee went to Cupar to discuss matters, they suggested that the hall might be better off back in local ownership. The District Council was unmoved, referring to the original feu contract with Lord Zetland and saying that 'under the deed of constitution the hall must remain the property of the District Council.' Anyway, Dunbog was surely behaving ungratefully; Cupar District Council could not see how it could possibly be to the locals' advantage to take responsibility, given that at present the Council paid the bills.

But that was the trouble: Cupar Council wasn't paying for anything much. In December 1948, a new and energetic minister arrived at Dunbog manse, and took over as chair of the hall committee. The Rev. Buchan had a gift for publicity, and on July 20th 1949 the *Courier & Advertiser* carried a report:

DUNBOG HALL COMPLAINTS

> When social functions are held in Dunbog Hall in the winter, residents have to take oil lamps with them. This was stated by Rev. Buchan who, with his session clerk Mr T. Watson, Johnston Farm, attended yesterday's meeting of Cupar District Council to ask that the hall should be given back to the people. The hall was handed over to the District Council 20 years ago. Mr Buchan said since then its condition has progressively deteriorated…Two dilapidated iron lamps are the only means of light, the heating system is dangerous, the woodwork is 'crying out' for paint, a new floor is needed, the roof needs repair, and a better water supply is required. The deputation asked that the District Council should foot the bill and then give back the ownership of the hall to local trustees so that it could be kept in good repair in future.

The District Council agreed, but grudgingly. They at first repeated that the feu contract meant the hall must stay in their final ownership. Nor did they want to meet the estimated £860 repairs bill, but would see if grants were available; perhaps the post-war 'Salute the Soldiers' fund would help. But, faced with the Rev. Buchan's badgering, by 1949 the Council had agreed to a full transfer; the major legal obstacles seemed to have evaporated, and would only require an approach to the feu superior (still Lord Zetland) and the Secretary of State for Scotland to secure consent.

Both gave that consent, although the estate was not going to relax any of the feu conditions, for example the prohibition on alcohol. (In January 1951, someone hiring the hall was reprimanded for raffling a bottle of whisky.)

In the meantime, the hall committee saw that they must improve the building to keep up with the times. There was still no sign of mains electricity in Dunbog, so in 1949 new oil lamps were installed, together with asbestos fire-proofing. They wanted to buy a 'Sussex' cooker using 'rural gas' (bottled) to replace the old range. They wanted a new floor, some proper concrete steps and an entrance gate, external and internal painting, the walls re-pointed, and the 'door of the present men's lavatory to be closed and a new entrance to be formed in the outer wall, avoiding access through the kitchen.' The WRI wanted better than that. They thought the present kitchen no kitchen at all, and wanted the renewal plan to include an extension. They would have to wait. Meanwhile the heating was to be overhauled, with new radiators and more of that useful asbestos.

The repairs could all be done for a much reduced budget of £448 5/7d. to be paid by the District Council before the handover. Work began, and was delayed, and began again... In frustration, the hall committee did what they could and bought six new ashtrays. But even as the work was completed, things went badly wrong. In December 1951 the hall caretaker, Mrs Walker, died suddenly. While the committee was looking for a replacement, no one remembered to drain the new radiators. They froze, and were wrecked.

Still the negotiations dragged on; the whole process took eight years. Finalising a new constitution took forever. Should the WRI be automatic trustees? What about the minister and Session clerk? Who would actually own the hall, and on whose behalf? At a committee meeting in 1951, we see them still fretting over the new constitution, worrying that 'a larger and more representative committee' was needed, even if it had taken a grant refusal to remind them of the parish women.

Did the people wish to be represented? In June 1951, a public meeting was called to consider the deal. It was (said the hall minutes) 'advertised in the *People's Journal*, and fully intimated.' Nineteen people attended, including a young Mr Dennis Currie, appointed as the new secretary. At this meeting, exasperation with the delays was apparent. The 'Scottish Home Office' was demanding on unclear legal grounds that the local trustees purchase the hall for £5; the constitution still wasn't right, and now Rev. Buchan took a huff. He 'expressed difficulties experienced by him in cooperating with the District Council' and, 'in view of references to him in a Council letter, he wished to withdraw as a trustee.' Mr Buchan had also stood down as hall chairman; he was the last Dunbog minister of the kirk to hold the chair.[67] A farmer, Thomas Watson, took over to try to haul the negotiations to a conclusion. In August, when yet another meeting was called to approve the constitution, only two parishioners turned up.

But the hall was back in the hands of the people.

1954: A new Deed of Trust

One last matter had to be settled before the formal handover could be completed: if the hall was to be in the control of local trustees, there would have to be a new Deed of Trust. This document was finally signed and recorded in August 1954.

The new trustees are listed: David Ferguson of Grange of Lindores; John Howie of Ballinbreich; Major George Fullerton-Carnegie of Aytounhill; Mrs Jean Lawson Gordon of Johnston, and the Scottish Council for Social Service. The Dunbog Kirk Session, the Women's Guild, and the WRI are given as ex-officio committee members. As before, Lord Zetland would be the feu superior, although this is not mentioned in the 1954 Deed. All the

---

[67] The last minister of Dunbog Kirk (to 1983) was Rev. Titterington, who had no role at the hall. His son Eric recalls: 'He wasn't interested. He had his hands far too full running two churches.'

original feu contract provisions still applied, including the ban on alcohol and on 'nauseous, troublesome and dangerous' activities. The new Deed maintains the high moral tone with loud and anachronistic echoes of early 19th century calls for 'rational recreation':

> '[Dunbog Hall is] dedicated and held by us and our successors as Trustees in all time coming for the purposes of physical and mental training, and social, moral and intellectual development through the medium of reading rooms, library, lectures, classes or otherwise as may be found expedient of the inhabitants of Dunbog in the County of Fife.'

Dunbog in the early 1950s

What was Dunbog like at this time, when people power was restored to the hall? The *Third Statistical Account of Scotland (County of Fife)* by Alexander Smith was published in 1952; it gives us a vivid picture. Dunbog and Flisk, wrote Smith, had the lowest population density of all parishes in Fife: just six people per 100 acres. The population was still largely (75%) engaged on the land one way or another: Ayton estate employed foresters, gamekeepers, market gardeners and a rabbit trapper. But (says Smith), increasing numbers of Dunbog workers were employed outside the parish; they were commuting to Dundee, to Perth, and to the quarry and the linoleum factory at Newburgh using Dunbog's overcrowded two-hourly bus service, 'inadequate for those who wish to travel.' They might previously have used the railway, which had closed to passenger traffic only the year before.[68] But perhaps it was too expensive and infrequent.

---

[68] The Dunbog bus was withdrawn also in 2014.

Glenduckie, *c*.1950. Aggie Brown's shop (with the tall chimney, centre). Behind it stands the doocot, still with its roof slates.

Facilities had declined. There had once been a sub-post office, a resident District Nurse, and shops at Sandyknowes and at Glenduckie where Davie Thomson now lives. As a boy, Davie minded the hens for Aggie Brown the shopkeeper, and was paid an apple a time. One afternoon she said, 'You've not had so much to do today,' sliced the apple and ate half. But the shops closed. There was not even a phone box. Few people had cars, though there was a taxi service at the Dunbog crossroads operated by a former chauffeur. In place of Aggie Brown, Smith wrote that 'Vans and lorries from neighbouring centres serve the housewife' – although ever since vans had become common in the 1930s, the health professions had complained that the supply of jam, pappy bread, tins and sugar were doing real harm to rural nutrition, especially to teeth.

Other aspects of Dunbog were rudimentary. Only the main road was paved. Most cottages relied on oil lamps, and on hand pumps or field supply for water.[69] In Abdie, a number were still thatched with reeds from the banks of the Tay.[70] The school 'now has its own dining hall and kitchen, but a lavatory system that is disgraceful in its primitiveness. The lack of water is given as the reason, but this would hardly seem to hold good with a burn running alongside.' Meanwhile, Smith reported that for Dunbog's minister, life was a struggle:

> There is a manse and garden of a size which, coupled with the lack of electricity and gas, and the difficulty of securing help, makes it most difficult for any minister to run them satisfactorily without detriment to his own and his wife's health and work… In winter, inclement weather and long distances are not conducive to regular worship, while summer is a period of hard work with little leisure…

Lack of modern water and electricity supplies plagued Dunbog:

> It seems very unjust that the agricultural population should not have the same amenities of electricity, water and sanitation, and at the same rates, as the town dwellers, whose lives are not so hard physically and who have cultural amenities denied to the rural parishes.

Of the hall itself, Smith wrote:

> The Parish Hall makes a centre for all kinds of activities, and serves fairly well to meet the needs of a rural area. It is used for Kirk functions, for meetings, for concerts, and for youth work. Sessions for country and modern dancing are also held, and Ministry of Information films are shown from time to time.

The School Log also records a brush with the movies; the Cinema Van visited to show *Animal Camouflage*, with *Land*

---

[69] Several cottages in Glenduckie are still using filtered field water in 2023.
[70] Reed thatching had been a modern improvement when the Tay reed beds were established in the 18th century. Reed made a better roof than turf, furze or bracken.

Behind the Dykes and *Pygmies of Africa*. But, for glamour, it was necessary to travel three miles to Newburgh where 'The Public Hall cinema is open three nights a week, and is well patronised.' Regretfully, Smith observed that 'The [Newburgh] Library is not used as it deserves, the billiard room being more popular.'

Examining the moral fibre of Dunbog's people in 1952, the *Third Account* confessed to that uncertainty first met in 1836: the agricultural population was still too mobile, 'with little opportunity to create a permanent interest in the life of the parish.' But all was not lost: the gentry were not so footloose, and were playing their part: 'The proprietor of Aytounhill[71] is the respected gentleman squire of the parish. He has nursed his estates, its forests and its farms with assiduous care, and spent much money to keep the whole in good order.' And there was hope for Dunbog's lower classes: 'There is a nucleus that remains more or less stationary. Of a fine moral quality, they owe much, perhaps, to the fact that their lives are simple and natural, free from the sophistication and artificiality so often characteristic of the city dweller.'

1954: Tentative expansion

The *Third Account*'s lukewarm remark that the hall 'serves fairly well to meet needs' is revealing: modernisation was long overdue. Once again, plans for an extension were drawn up, and architects – Mills & Shepherd, of Cupar – were consulted. But where to find the money? The architect's first plans were costed at £2,200. The committee, recovering from the shock, asked for something that could be done for £1,200. There was about £400 in the bank. Funds must be raised, but local activities could not do it alone: a recent Harvest Home supper had brought in just £49 14/1d. So

---

[71] Major George Fullerton-Carnegie. The family had built Aytounhill House in 1876 and bought a number of farms with cottages, including Aytoun, Glenduckie, Denmuir, Balmeadie and Balmeadowside. Almost all are now owner-occupied. The Fullerton-Carnegies sold off their Dunbog estates soon after the *Third Account* was published.

some of the trustees stepped forward: Mr Watson and Mr Stirrat both offered loans of £50. Major Fullerton-Carnegie had also said he would help. And at last, Fife Council agreed a loan of £110.

Aytounhill House lochan c.1950. This had been created when the new 'big house' was built in 1876.

But the thing must be done properly, or they'd not get the money and might even be breaking the law; the minutes for May 1955 remark intriguingly that the improvements must include 'the additional urinal and toilet we were duty bound to provide as per conditions of grant aid and local burgh police act.' Poor toilets had spurred the improvement plan of 1949.[72] Although there would still be oil lamps, the new extension should be future-proofed by including 'fittings for electricity', while perhaps better water could be brought from the supply at Balmeadie cottages along the road.

---

[72] When the hall sought a large grant for the 2003 improvements, installing a disabled access toilet was one of the conditions.

There should of course be a decent heating system.[73] (Heating problems dogged the hall; the accounts show the radiators split by frost being sold as scrap for £1 4/- while a new set of duties for the hall keeper specifies, in frosty weather, the draining of all the pipes, pump and boiler, the mains tap turned off, and anti-frost heaters lit in the toilets.)

But if they wanted to extend, there was a problem: in which direction to build? To the south there was a road; to the west there was no land free. To the east there was a ditch. To the north, the ground was too wet. The problem was solved by the Zetland estate who, in 1954, granted a tiny patch of extra land to the west (the school side) to accommodate a new kitchen, allowing the utility space at the east end to be reworked as decent male and female toilets behind the stage. These eventually became the rooms that now provide storage for chairs and for the After School Club's equipment. The additional space seems modest now, but this was the first development of the hall since 1914, half a century before.

The precise proposals and alterations are difficult to deduce from the sketchy comments in the hall minutes, which never specify exactly what work was planned or carried out, or at what date. Detailed reporting was reserved for a new crisis, as related in the minutes of the committee meeting of May 1955:

> The secretary [Dennis Currie] reported that the hall keeper was insisting that several patrons and committees using the hall who had been using the few [coat] hooks provided in the kitchen should be prevented from doing so. In his opinion this was contrary to police regulations. Mr Currie suggested that it was for the management to decide who was to use these hooks. It was agreed that use be confined to committees of organisations using the kitchen, and that a notice to this effect be affixed to the door.
>
> The hall keeper in view of the foregoing offered his

---

[73] At this time the cellar was dug and a coal-fired boiler installed below the new kitchen. This boiler gave up quickly; by 1967 it was already rusted. The cellar was often awash with rainwater and would not drain properly.

resignation, but this the committee did not accept, in view of the triviality of the case. Mr Watson stated that we were not in a position in such a small rural community to be too rigid with rules, and we should be moderate in our regulations.

This is the last item in the 1936-55 minute book.

1955-67: the doldrums

On the first page of a new foolscap minute book (June 1955), Dennis Currie added the role of hall treasurer to his position as secretary. Finding anyone to take an interest in the hall was a problem which, over the next decade, would become a crisis beyond coat hooks. This, and the ever-greater financial difficulties, make the next decade of hall minutes rather sad reading.

The AGM of 1956 sets the tone: Mr Watson in the chair 'welcomed the few who were present'. The money concerns never cease; fuel is expensive, repaying the Cupar Council building loan is a heavy burden, the hall keeper's wages are a trouble, and income from letting is only £37 14/6d. The fuel bill in 1956 covers coke, wood and gas, but in 1957 there is an electricity bill as well – so at least mains power had finally reached Dunbog. The committee resolves to write to Cupar Council to request a reduction in the rates, while Mr Bethune – 'our mainstay in the entertainments' – is asked to 'try to form a new committee to raise funds.' There was a clear need now for a proper car park, but the slip of land at the back of the hall was a mess. Mr Watson and Mr Currie would 'try to enlist voluntary labour to level out the rubble.'

There were some signs of life: connection to the water mains in 1958 was another improvement. Certain activities continued come what may: whist drives were held fortnightly, with the children playing dominoes up on the stage while their parents dealt the cards. The social club behind these evenings could make a donation of £24 10/- to the Hall Trust in 1963. Mr Watson 'promised to try to get a concert party.' The school was still using the hall, paying all of £5 per annum but at least keeping it under supervision. In 1965, unsupervised youth were causing the committee grief with their nauseous, troublesome and dangerous activities:

> An application from the local youth club to use the space over the stage for storage purposes was unanimously rejected on the grounds that in view of the conduct of the club and damage already done, it would be too great a risk to allow access to the loft.

The committee urgently needed to find more income. In 1958 they had recorded the 'serious financial position' with reserves 'very low'. In 1959, 'It was noted that the financial position was very acute but it was decided to wait until the autumn before trying to raise some funds by entertainments.' In 1960, with the WRI 'finished', the letting prospects were 'bad', and the rates payable to the District Council hung on the hall like an albatross: 'The treasurer was requested to intimate to the auditors that at present we are unable to pay.' In 1961 –

> Mr Bethune pointed out that all the money we were raising for hall funds was being absorbed by the local rates and he felt that it was unjust that we should raise money just to pay rates.

They were driven to asking favours, and expressed 'the committee's gratitude to the blacksmith Mr McKenzie for the fine job he had made in repairing the boiler of the heating system, all free of charge.' Which was fortunate, because they had abandoned a proposed lottery for lack of interest.

In the face of these difficulties, morale sank low. At the 1958 AGM the chairman expresses 'disappointment at the poor turn out'. In 1959 he is disappointed again; the committee are the only people present. When, in 1960, Mr Watson announced his retirement from the committee, he must have felt sad at the state of affairs; he had served for three decades. (The parish clearly felt the significance of the moment; neighbours chipped in for an oak bureau for Mr Watson, and a silver platter for Mrs Watson.) But it got worse. At the AGM in 1962, just three people were present. The spring AGM for 1967 was aborted; only Mr Bethune and Mr Currie were there, and down in the cellar the heating boiler was playing up again.

They tried again for an AGM in October 1967 and (understandably), 'The secretary intimated Mr Bethune's wish to retire from his post as chairman due to health reasons on advice from his doctor.' It was time to face the grim question:

> It was put to those present – would we wind up the hall's affairs or would we try to carry on. It was proposed by Mrs McKenzie that we carry on for another year to see if we can justify keeping the hall open as everyone thought it would be a pity to let it close.

If the hall had closed its doors in 1967, under the terms of the 1914 feu contract the building and land would have reverted to Lord Zetland's estate. In the meantime:

> The secretary reported that the boiler was now almost u/s, leaking, and the smoke box rusted and burnt out, and could not be relied on to heat the hall. It was unanimously agreed that we proceed to get estimates for heating by electricity.

But, to keep their spirits up:

> Concert party: Mr Lumsden to try for Happy Wanderers in December.

Two other things kept Dunbog amused during these years: the Highland games, and the zoo. The games were held in the 1950s in the grounds of Aytounhill; a charabanc (with wooden benches) shuttled people up from as far as Newburgh.

Meanwhile, Tom Spence had taken on the tenancy of Dunbog farm after his father Bert (lamb and offal king of the pre-war years). Tom – born in Newburgh – was a qualified vet, and had a keen interest in exotic birds. At Dunbog he also kept wallabies, monkeys, and a cheetah called Puss Puss which he would take in his Jaguar to go shopping in Cupar, on a lead. The fame of the Dunbog cheetah spread, and the BBC came to film it running down a hare on the hillside – but instead of going for the hare, Puss Puss turned on the nearby sheep. Trying to separate them, Tom Spence was mauled.

Tom Spence and Puss Puss

Spence left Dunbog in 1967, moving to Perth (Australia) to run the city zoo there. But this was not the last of the cats. In July 1998, the *Daily Record* reported the experience of another farmer, Bill Carswell. Returning from an evening out, he'd come face to face with a puma, 'terrifying' and 'bulging with muscle'. The puma fled the scene; the farmer gave chase 'at forty m.p.h.' but lost the quarry. The Fife Ranger Service confirmed that the paw-prints were indeed puma-size, and the investigating police recalled the existence of the zoo thirty years before, noting that when Tom

Spence had gone to Australia, no one knew what had become of Puss Puss.[74]

The ending of the games, and the closure of both Dunbog zoo and the railway were followed by further blows. The shrinking congregations of Dunbog and Abdie Kirks were amalgamated in 1965, and Dunbog Kirk could not survive.[75] When the committee considered closing the hall in 1967, they may have wondered what would be left of the old community life. Even the 'respected gentleman squire' of the parish was gone. For years, landed estates had found it difficult to make satisfactory profits from farm rents. By mid-century, many had had enough, and were selling farms to tenants or to investors. The Fullerton-Carnegies sold Glenduckie farm in 1959, with Bealmeadie, Ayton and Denmuir farms going at much the same time. The process continued steadily, and in 1982 the Dundas (Zetland) family would sell their last landholding in Scotland, the entire Flisk estate of farms including Higham, Dunbog, and Johnston, which they had acquired in 1762. Back then it had been called 'the Lands and Barony of Ballinbreich.' Now Dunbog parish land was to be owned not by feudal landlords but by the people who farmed it.[76] The old patriarchy was ending also.

What did the landed families think of severing the connection? The Fullerton-Carnegies seem to have been more interested in their properties in Switzerland. One day in 1969, in their absence, Aytounhill House burned down; an electrical fault was blamed.[77] The squire's family never returned to Dunbog.

---

[74] A 1985 obituary in *The West Australian* says that Spence took Puss Puss with him to Australia by ship, with the cheetah enjoying sitting up on the bridge with the captain.

[75] Rev. Titterington preached a last service in 1983, when Abdie & Dunbog linked to Newburgh. The kirk was sold, and became a private home in 1994.

[76] When the hall was built in 1914, just 11% of Scottish farms were owner occupied. This rose sharply after WW1. Large estates owned 2/3^{rds} of Fife's farmland in 1870, but only 1/3rd by 1970. (Callander, 1987).

[77] A new house was built at Aytonhill some thirty years after the fire by Neil Findlay.

Aytounhill House, home of the Fullerton-Carnegies.

1967-1999: Staying alive

1967 was the nadir, the darkest hour of Dunbog Hall. The decline had come about over little more than a decade; it is sad to think that it was precisely that decade in which local people had re-assumed ownership. Thereafter, the institution came to life but only slowly, and on several later occasions its survival was in doubt.

That it did survive was due in part to two factors: the Community Council, and Dennis Currie.

Parish Councils and Community Councils have come and gone in various guises. The Dunbog records include a blue A4 notebook, which contains handwritten minutes from another iteration of the Community Council in 1977 – after the abolition of parishes as a Scottish government administrative unit in 1975.

The minutes are careful and formal, and one decision of the first meeting was that Council meetings should be held every three months. At the next meeting they sensibly resolved that twice a year would be quite enough.

Discussions in 1977 dealt with many concerns: a little girl at Dunbog school who had diabetes was not getting adequate care from the Fife catering service, and what would we do about that? Traffic on the main road was dangerous for the school children, and how might that be tackled? Might the school janitor be given a 'lollipop'? But no: who would cover the insurance? There was annoyance that Fife Council seemed to dedicate no money to repairing the awful state of the village side roads. And pensioners were finding it difficult travelling to Grange of Lindores to collect their "bus tokens", so an arrangement was made for them to collect from Dunbog Hall.

Children's picnics organised by the Community were to be encouraged, as they promoted unity. Someone thought there was gold in the local hills. In 1979, someone else wanted to re-open Glenduckie quarry. One of the old railway bridges looked in danger of collapsing. The tenant at Grange Terrace No.1 had been evicted, 'after village people had become very worried about his actions.' In 1981, the Royal wedding (Charles and Diana) would be noted but there should be no 'special decor' in the parish. A commemorative tree was vandalised. An organisation called Community Industry would be helping to build the Hall extension (a dour windowless attachment containing a bar). In 1985 there is correspondence from the 'Campaign for a Scottish Assembly'. There was the closure of Dunbog kirk: what should happen to the bell and the stained-glass? It was suggested these should be moved to the Hall (but they went to Abdie kirk instead). Dutch Elm Disease was spreading, and people were advised to keep a watch out for it. There was concern that 'tinkers' had settled by Macduff Cottage[78] (and would the police please move them on? Yes, the police did so). Local public transport was poor, and the post-bus

---

[78] A thatched cottage at Lindores, currently under a corrugated shelter.

was an inadequate solution, as it took so long to get anywhere. There was annoyance that the Post Office was insisting on including Newburgh in Dunbog addresses, as this often led to letters going astray in Newburgh. There were questions about the Library Bus, and would the service be maintained? (In 2000, the library bus was still visiting weekly, parking in Glenduckie mainly for the benefit of Mrs Lawson at Castlehill cottage). Rights of way were being mapped, and in January 1988 the Community Council noted 'the forthcoming poll tax'.

Thus the Council, for all that it lacked any teeth or policy powers, maintained some sense of community opinion and consensus.

Dennis Currie's name appears in Community Council discussions, but he had also become Hall secretary on joining the committee in 1951. In some ways, Dennis exemplified the old stereotype of the static community. He had been born in 1926 at Balmeadie cottages, moving less than a mile to Glenduckie when he married in 1951, and never leaving. His family were not farm workers (and were thus less likely to move on): his father Charles, who had served as hall keeper before WW2, had been a forester on the Ayton estate. Dennis himself was a railwayman, based not on the Newburgh & North Fife but working at Cupar and then Dundee. For some years there was an old railway lamp post outside the family house.

Over the period 1966 to 1999, minutes from meetings of the Hall committee are erratic, with some gaps of several years. But there are correspondence files covering each year up to the Millennium, and these show Dennis Currie keeping the essential business moving with doggedness and attention to detail. It is a remarkable record. Year in, year out, the correspondence records Dennis dealing with everything that arises:

– purchasing seventy-two second-hand tubular steel chairs.

– negotiating with the Council the maximum capacity of the
hall, which was set at 160 closely seated, 114 dancing, or 73 for

a dinner.

– obtaining a grant to replace rotting windows.

– beer and coffee stains on the vaulting horse, caused by the band at a dance

– dancers damaging the floor by sprinkling it with salt instead of ballroom polish.

– a break-in by boys from Melville House School at Collesie (an institution for problem youth, now closed).

– vandalism (passers-by on the road; no one was caught).

– waste collection, 'consisting mainly of party debris and floor sweepings'.

– leaking pipes at the roadside, and a dispute with the Council as to whose fault it was. This happened twice.

– insurance, and should this include cover against riot?

– purchasing a new stainless steel sink (Dennis had seen a 'world beating offer' in the local press).

– hot water in the toilets. This last illustrated a poor fit between official and local expectations. The hall had been informed by Fife Council that this was now a requirement of any place seeking a 'license for public amusement'. Dennis objected in writing:

> Cold water, soap and towels are provided, and we have had no complaints from patrons. We feel your advisers should reconsider their recommendations, especially bearing in mind that this is a rural area and our resources are very limited.

The Council was unimpressed by his arguments, but did offer a grant to help pay for installation work.

Glenduckie, 2014. Dennis Currie lived in the white house, with his wife Chrissie and their sons. Previously it had been two homes, one the residence of the District Nurse. In the mid-19th.c it had also contained a small school. It has more recently been extensively renovated by two young architects who live there.

Dennis Currie kept a tight control over the accounts. Anyone hiring the hall was liable for the precise amount of electricity consumed; Dennis would read the meter before the function, and read it again afterwards; the bill would be exact. The school was, in Dennis's opinion, extravagant with the electricity. They were using the hall more frequently, and leaving the electric heaters on. But the heaters (suspended from the ceiling) were inefficient and slow to warm the space, leading to the school complaining to Fife Council that the hall was often too cold to use. It was at least agreed that each unit consumed would be recorded by the head teacher and paid for. Payments to the Hall now attracted the interest of H.M.Inspector of Taxes in Cupar. Dennis claimed that the hall was a charity, and thus exempt from taxes – but the taxman wanted to know: on whose authority? Dennis was embarrassed to confess that 'the correspondence I have only goes back to 1966,' but that 'I am of the mind that our trust were favoured with a charitable status back in the 1940s.'[79]

One exchange of letters marked a shift in social norms. In 1976, the school's parent-teacher association wished to hold a dance, and to provide a cash bar. But the feu contract forbidding alcohol was still in force. Dennis wrote to the Zetland's solicitors asking for permission to sell drinks at the dance. He noted that:

> So far as I am aware, no such application has ever been made before in the history of the Hall, and I, as responsible Manager, would not like to think that a precedent would be created if such a request was granted.

The estate agreed to the request, strictly as a one-off. With the bit between his teeth, Dennis wrote again:

> My Committee feel that in this modern age this clause [prohibiting alcohol] should be waived as an adequate safeguard is contained in the Public Amusement license.

Again, the feu superior agreed. That was the last of prohibition in Dunbog.[80] It was good timing, because the following year there was something to celebrate: the Queen's Silver Jubilee. A tree was planted at Aytounhill to match the Coronation Tree of 1953, which could be seen by the parish football field between the hall and Balmeadie. A dance was held, with a barbecue in a marquee outside and (thanks to the Zetland's change of heart) a bar. A great

---

[79] There was no Trust in the 1940s; the Trust dates from 1954. Dennis was perhaps recalling vaguely the hall's status as an offshoot of Dunbog Kirk, which had been a legal charity since 1904. Dunbog Hall was granted charitable status in its own right in January 2007.

[80] Although it was not the end of the issue. Today, the hall committee must apply for a bar license for each event, and there is a limit to the number of such licenses granted in one year.

bonfire was lit on Moonzie Hill and, to fund the celebrations, local farmers donated the proceeds from the sale of either one ton of barley or two fat lambs. There was no official involvement.[81]

Fife Council – perhaps aware that rural life and the rural economy were still fragile – tried to make amends with a string of grant schemes to halls and communities, and by offering a support network. As early as 1966, Dunbog delegates were called to a conference of village hall committees at Freuchie (and in 1967, this conference debated the old obsession with alcohol). The support network would go through many permutations with, for instance, a Federation of North East Fife Halls founded in 1994.

Some of the other support offered seems unreal. In 1982, the body called Community Industry (based at Cardenden) wrote to the hall committee:

ATTENTION ALL VOLUNTARY ORGANISATIONS

COMMUNITY INDUSTRY COULD BE THE ANSWER TO SOLVING SOME OF YOUR FINANCIAL PROBLEMS.

They offered training in money-minting activities, including *(sic)*:

MAKING OF SOFT TOYS AND HOUSEHOLD ARTICLES I.E. OVEN GLOVES, TEA COSY'S, PINAFORES, PEG BAGS ETC. FOR RESALE.

Pinafores and peg begs did not catch on in Dunbog.

Amongst other activities, in the 1970s the Council began to sponsor 'further education' projects in village halls; at Dunbog, one such was an art class taught by Mr Watt. The files record nothing of this other than some small administrative details, and it is not related whose idea it was to have Mr Watt paint the glorious mountain, lake and forest landscape covering the entire wall behind the stage. It is still there today, signed *Watt '71* and looking

---

[81] At least, not that I find recorded. Strangely, there is no mention of any aspect of this event in either the committee minutes (which at this date are sketchy) or the correspondence files. Thanks to Michael Struthers for his account.

like a cross between the Alps and the Canadian Rockies.

Mr Watt's mural

In the aftermath of the Silver Jubilee, another building renovation was funded by Fife Council grants. The kitchen was extended, the toilets renovated (again), and a permanent bar installed. The alterations created space but were unimaginative. With no window and fake wood walls, the new bar area was dark and unappealing.[82] Even then, there was some resistance, and a suggestion that bars didn't need windows; someone might look in and see you drinking. If they had looked in, they might have seen mishaps in the bar. Dennis Currie wrote to Fife Council:

> Dear Sir, My committee would like to undertake a major remedial repair in our hall, *viz.* raising the level of the annex floor. This annex was built by Community Services of Lochgelly, unfortunately, they got their levels wrong

---

[82] Inserting a window was discussed by the committee in 2001.

with the result, the floor level of the annex is some three inches lower than that of the hall resulting in a number of people falling over.

The children's play garden at the hall (2013).

It would be untrue to suggest that Dennis Currie was unsupported in all this work, even if he did provide the resilient spine of the committee. There was still a hall caretaker, although there was a limit to what could be expected there; responding to the complaint from the school about the feeble heating, Dennis informed Fife Council that the caretaker was paid 'less in a year than the school cleaner is paid in a week.'[83] It was still dispiritingly difficult to recruit helpers, and the minutes speak of committee members agreeing to carry on 'due to the lack of anyone else in the community coming forward'. In October 1974, seven years after

---

[83] Current legislation makes it very difficult to employ a caretaker, as the hall would be liable for e.g. National Insurance contributions which it could not afford, and administrative paperwork which it could not tolerate.

that despondent meeting when closure was first considered, another meeting faced the same awful question – and again they resolved to carry on.

Now other names start to appear regularly in the hall minutes: McKenzie, Struthers, Henderson, and more. Jock McKenzie of Ayton smiddy became chairman in 1977 and was still serving in 1992, when yet another 'relaunch committee' was formed. With each of these relaunches, programmes of entertainment and other uses were discussed. The 'winter programme' for 1990/1 was up-beat:

> 26/10/90 Whist drive
> 2/11/90   Dance – Paddy Neary [Irish accordionist]
> 28/12/90 Dance – band to be fixed
> 15/2/91   Tartan night
> 15/3/91   Dance – band to be fixed
> 12/4/91   Whist drive

Some proposed activities were unacceptable: 'The secretary had been approached to let the hall each week for dog training. The party had been refused use of the Institute in Newburgh.' They were refused Dunbog also, on grounds of food hygiene.

By 1999, there is a weary air to the correspondence files, weighed down as they are with forms regarding grants, rebates, bills, licensesfor entertainments, and insurance payments. By this date, Dennis Currie had served on the committee for nearly half a century since 1951. Other committee members were tiring also. Dennis knew that he needed help, and needed someone to relievehim of the work. He looked around the community, and thought of consulting with the Trustees appointed when the hall had been taken back into community ownership in 1954.

The Trustees were all dead. Something had to be done.

Dunbog Hall c.1999 (north side)

The hall at its most glum, with the windowless 1982 bar and store on the right. The just visible steps lead to the rear door; the front entrance is still the roadside porch. In 1999 the committee sent this photo to Dulux when applying for a grant of free paint, which they didn't get.

2000: Millenium rebirth

For only the third time in the hall's history, April 1999 saw a full new set of Trustees appointed, and a new committee formed also. Dennis Currie remained as treasurer in the short term, but had made it clear that he intended to step down soon.[84] The new chairman was the owner of Dunbog Farm, Billy Harvey, and he was clear what the first duty of the committee should be: a memorable Hogmanay ceilidh to mark the Millennium.

Comparing the minutes of committee meetings in 1999 with those a decade or two earlier, the air of discipline and

---

[84] He retired in 2001, after fifty years. Dennis died in 2012.

determination is striking. Meetings were now large: ten or eleven members might be there, numbers unheard of for many years. The 1999 meetings were frequent: April, May, June, September, November and December – again, something that had not been seen in recent memory. There was a palpable anxiety that the Millennium party should go without any hitch. Every smallest aspect was discussed repeatedly, and carefully minuted: the purchase of cutlery, a radio for the bells, a tape-recorder to play reels, and should Reverend Logan say Grace? And how to suspend balloons from the ceiling, and who would provide sparklers for the children, and should the children each be presented with a commemorative scroll? It was proposed that 'the oldest citizen of Dunbog might be invited to say a few words just before midnight.' But, on due consideration, it was agreed that 'the longest resident' should be asked: Dennis Currie, of course.

Even from just fifteen years' distance, the tone of the discussion now seems firmly of its time. They debated 'the possibility of installing a TV set in the hall in order to share the final moments of the 20th century with the many Scots assembled in Princes Street in Edinburgh.' There was to be Bothy Ballad singing – but there was a problem: 'A pianist to accompany the singing would be a great advantage,' says the May minutes, but 'does anyone know of a local pianist?' (One imagines the incredulity of the 1930s WRI, with their piano social evenings.) At the Millennium party, there was even to be 'a gas Heater and a Telephone' provided outside.

The minutes show a nagging uncertainty as to whether they should risk going ahead with the party at all; was there any community interest? It is as though someone had asked: is there a community? Abdie Hall had timorously cancelled their Millennium party for fear of lack of takers. A final 'Dunbog decision day' of 1st November was declared – and when it came, there was relief: ticket sales were going well, the target of 100 was sure to be reached. In the event, three long tables the length of the hall were packed for a stovie supper.

There were bothy ballads and dancing and young Kyle Noble of Glenduckie played the fiddle. A net heaped with balloons had been strung right across the hall above the tables, and as midnight rang out the net was drawn back so that the balloons poured down. There was a splendid Millennium Cake[85] featuring an icing sugar hall beside an icing sugar Norman's Law. The event created such euphoria that a press release was issued afterwards to say what a very fine evening it had been.

Thereafter, a cooler realism returned. The press release acknowledged that, apart from the school's activities, 'the hall has not been much used in the recent past.'

And the realities of commitment returned. At a meeting on the 10th January 2000, Billy Harvey the chairman said that he was busy with his farm, and could not sustain the sort of effort the Millennium had required. But continued events were most

---

[85] Made by Barry Batchelor, a professional caterer living in the parish.

important, he said, so how could they be ensured? Considering the finances, Major Innes suggested that 'a letter be sent around the Community explaining the importance of the hall and calling for a one-time financial donation' – but they thought better of that. A programme was drawn up of fund-raising and social evenings: Burns Night, St Andrews Night, and a Summer Adult Dance, a silent auction and a Jazz Night. It was not so dissimilar to the programmes of the 1980s, the 50s and the 30s.

Almost in passing, 'it was agreed that the hall might be easier to let if it was modernised.'

At this time, a protracted wrangle had developed over planning permission for a house to be built next door, on land between the hall and the school. The problem hinged on access. Fife Council had said that permission could not be given for a third access road; that was too many on a fast highway. So, a common access for the hall and the new house was proposed, the house developer to pay any legal costs. But for the hall there was a practical difficulty: the new access would now come to the back of the building, and not to the front porch by the road.

So, beginning with the notion of moving the main entrance round to the back, the idea of another redevelopment of the building took hold: was it not time to modernize more radically? And while one was about it, this really was the moment for a disabled toilet, and far more storage. And how about a decent heating system at last? The first plan drawn up in 2001 by Major Innes, the secretary, shows the hall entrance moved to the rear, with a large new storage annex. The combined floor area would now be a third larger than the original building.

At this time, however, Luthrie Hall nearby had just undergone an extensive renovation. They had been successful in obtaining a large National Lottery grant, and had made their building fit with the needs of their school for recreation and for classes, and also as a kitchen and dining room. Not only had the structure been extensively altered, but every aspect of Luthrie Hall had been assessed from the point of view of the disabled, the partially sighted, the hard of hearing, the elderly, and children. Every sign was in strong contrasting colours with Braille besides. Every door handle was accessible to a wheelchair user. Every door hinge was shielded from small fingers. The Dunbog committee clearly had to think on a more detailed, bigger, and more imaginative scale.

It was a time-consuming and elaborate process. An architect was found to produce detailed drawings for planning approval. To the National Lottery, the Dunbog committee submitted over eighty pages of documentation for a grant application, including the feu contract and trust deeds, a new 'disability assessment' and an 'anti-discrimination policy'. In the early autumn of 2002, there came a letter saying that Dunbog had won a provisional grant of £138,000.

But the excitement was mixed with dismay when tenders from three builders arrived, all well over that amount. Dunbog could not ask the Lottery to raise the award, which was only valid for one year. Nor was it allowed to cut corners, because then the specification would have changed and the grant would lapse. Extra money had to be found in a hurry – and only after urgent telephoning, form filling and badgering could enough support be gathered from a combination of Fife Council, LEADER (E.U.), the TSB, and the Gannochy, Robertson, and Russell Trusts.

Lastly, there was a grant to enable decorative works; these would include the marking out of the floor for games, and also panels of clay fitted to the exterior either side of the front door, made by the school children supervised by the artist Kyra Clegg from Newburgh. They show scenes and faces from Dunbog, Glenduckie, Ayton and Denmuir; the identity of one, a bearded man, has never been established.

In the middle of all this, the Lottery declared that the architect was insufficiently qualified; they would not pay any money if he continued in post. The hurriedly-found replacement, Bill Armstrong, was very well qualified; he had been one of the team attempting to keep the Holyrood parliament building project under control, and had resigned when the MSPs' additional demands pushed the costs to ever greater heights. He succeeded in completing the Dunbog renovations under budget, though dogged by problems. Sighing over the difficulties, Bill Armstrong said one day: 'I thought that when I died they would find 'Holyrood' engraved upon my bleeding heart – but it will be 'Dunbog'.'

The hall closed for the renovations in the autumn of 2002, and the builder – John Simpson of Newburgh – began his careful work. Almost to the last, the old building sprang tricks and surprises.

Decorative tiles by the schoolchildren, installed by the new front door (2003)

Health regulations required the bar to have not one sink for washing glasses, but three, and there was not enough room. The heating engineers having installed a new oil-fired system, it was found that hot water to the kitchen had been forgotten; they had to cut a hole in the floor and crawl underneath with piping. A plan to position a cold water tank in the loft was abandoned when the structural engineer declared that the roof beams would not support it. The work was nearly finished when Bill Armstrong telephoned:

'Were you thinking of holding an opening party? If so, don't invite me. I think the old ceiling plaster is about to fall.' It had to be replaced, at the cost of another £7,000.

The hall re-opened in the spring of 2003 with a party and (in a faint echo of Lord Zetland's patronage) a speech by Robert Spencer Nairn, Lord Lieutenant of Fife. It was in time for the new school year. The building looked much as it does today, complete with a neat set of stage lights to add to the drama. All that was needed to be bang up to date was solar water heating and a music system. And now we have those too.

The Path

Before the hall's centenary arrived, another significant change was proposed. The Fife Coastal Path, running the full 117-mile length of our shore, had been opened in stages and by 2008 was almost complete; only a last few miles from Balmerino to Newburgh remained to be established with a route around Norman's Law and Glenduckie hill, possibly passing right through Glenduckie itself. The hall committee was approached by Fife Rangers with a proposal: the Council was already planning a new footpath linking the school to the Glenduckie lane to provide a safer walking route for schoolchildren. How would it be if this was extended to the hall car park, allowing users of the Coastal Path somewhere to leave cars and with a point of access to the walk? There was a presentation by the Rangers; maps were spread out in the hall and considered. The Coastal route might go almost past my front door (I envisaged selling teas) and Dunbog Hall would become a point on a nationally important footpath; the old 'rational recreation' reformers would surely have approved.

But any matter involving changes to hall property had to be referred to the trustees, and in September 2008 they turned it down. There were practical difficulties: a bridge would be required over the burn, and at several times of day the car park was crowded with school traffic anyway. But there was also a consideration that recalled Dunbog's isolated history: a fear of attracting too many visitors, of becoming a honey pot. One trustee argued that his lane was already plagued by walkers leaving cars when heading for Norman's Law. So permission was refused (and the walkers leave their cars in the Glenduckie-Higham lane instead).

In 1914, any Council hoping to establish such a path would have had to negotiate with just two landowners: Dundas (Zetland) and Carnegie (Aytoun); the farms on these estates would have done as they were instructed. By 2008, each farm was owner-occupied and had to be approached individually. Not all were keen, and so parts of the Coastal Path took a tortuous route out of sight of the water. By Higham, however, it is back on course and following the line of the ancient road that can be seen on Ainslie's map of 1775,[86] along the hills safely above the old marsh of Dunbog.

In 2014 there was talk of raising funds to purchase farmland beside the hall for a 'Community Park and playing field', reviving the former parish football field, and linking to the Coastal Pathway after all.

Dunbog 2014 and beyond

A rural parish is never the stable, tranquil and unchanging picture of the fond imagination. The tiny community of Dunbog has mutated in unpredictable ways, and the land economy too, from cattle floundering in a marsh to a cheetah chasing cameramen on the hills, with forests, quarries, railways, pheasant shoots, and organic vegetables all passing by. With each shift in the surrounding society, a community hall must adapt if it is to survive.

---

[86] The map is reproduced in Taylor and on the NLS maps website.

In the aftermath of the 2003 renovations, many new uses have been considered and tried. A youth club never quite got off the ground, but then a population this size doesn't have so many youths. For a couple of years there was an active badminton group, but possibly we've grown older and stiffer. Other ideas for

Dunbog Hall 2014

regular sessions – monthly talks and discussions, chess and bridge evenings, and a youth band – have come and gone; often, the lack of a 'critical mass' of population has hindered them. Dunbog Hall has, however, accommodated regular Community Council meetings, jazz festivals, ceilidhs, school musicals, orienteering competitors, spinners and weavers, birthdays, weddings and family reunions, a Curlers Court, carol singers, a book club and an antiques evening. One winter the hall ran a 'race night' with films projected onto the wall and manic gambling by an excited crowd. Three years later another race night was offered – and nobody bought tickets.[87] But the annual summer games have been revived, and Dunbog's Hogmanay party is always the best in Fife. In June

---

[87] This was at the height of the 'credit crunch' and the banking crisis; gambling went out of fashion, briefly.

2014, a party for two hundred was held to celebrate the Centenary; an apple tree was planted, a time capsule placed in the hall roof.

Dunbog persists in long-range charity; just as, in the 17th century, the parish sent money to help a Fife seaman held captive in Algiers, so in the 21st century the committee has assisted sex workers in Ethiopia learning to make chocolates.[88] The school, meanwhile, formed strong links to a primary school in Malawi. Nor has local generosity failed. When Neil Findlay (of Aytounhill) died, he bequeathed the hall £2000 which has been spent on a new doorway and wooden steps out into the play garden, with a plaque carrying his name.

In practice, the school remains the chief client of Dunbog Hall, using it for meals, plays, gym, Dunbog's Got Talent, and the Harvest Tea. In 2014-15, on a wave of popular success and high reputation attracting families outside the catchment area, the school roll reached the extraordinary figure of 70 pupils, a crowd not seen there since the 19th century, and which would not be possible without the hall. In the afternoons, another use reflected current economics and demography: working families needed an After School Club. At Dunbog, this was run for some years in the hall every weekday, with paid staff but managed by a committee of parents, providing a service for each other that was not envisaged in 1914. But in 2018 the Club closed, unable to find a manager. We saw in 1923, in 1952 and in later decades that there was a only small pool of people available to take on community roles, sometimes doubling or trebling their duties as secretary, chairman, teacher or treasurer. That is true today; a few dozen familiar names rotate between the hall committee, the Community Council, and the Parents Council.

Our society is still changing, and Dunbog is now relatively affluent. The 2021 Census and other statistics[89] tell us the following about Abdie & Dunbog Community Council area:

---

[88] Through Barry Batchelor, and Women At Risk (WAR), an enterprise promoting alternative incomes.
[89] The figures are taken from the *Know Fife* database as at June 2023.

Population: 514. We have a higher proportion of women, and a lower proportion of children than the Fife average. The ten houses at Glenduckie have (in 2023) nine young children.

Home ownership: 72%. The Fife average is 61%.

Children living in poverty: 12%. The Fife average is 17%.

Economic deprivation and unemployment: 5%. The Fife average is 12%.

Car ownership: Only 11% of Dunbog households have no car, compared to 26% for all of Fife. But it would be increasingly difficult to live here without a car, given the lack of public transport.

Fife as a whole scores badly against all Scotland in figures for common assault and free school meals, but does better for female binge drinking, active travel to school, and for people saying this is a good place to live.

It is clearly no longer true that 75% of the working population is tied to agriculture. In Glenduckie – once a hamlet of farm cottages – there is today not a single farm labourer. No longer do the ploughmen move farm each year, although the population is still transitory: of the ten homes in Glenduckie, eight have changed occupants in the last ten years.[90] But nor are we all commuters; the rural-urban distinctions have blurred. Several farms, the greater part of their lands sold to larger neighbours, have shrunk to a small acreage that can support a modest number of animals, managed part-time by people with other professions.

Occupations have changed year by year: at Aytounhill, where there was once a stable block with farm workers in the bothy, there came instead a business selling horse tack, and a taxi service. In other homes we have had: a joiner married to a St Andrews academic; a dealer in farm machinery contracts who then became a financial advisor working from the old Glenduckie quarry; a

---

[90] 2013-23.

jeweller; a horse breeder and trainer; a supervisor on the tourist trains to the Highlands; a glass engraver; a financial manager flying each week to a job in London; a press photographer; a doctor; IT managers and others driving to Perth, St Andrews, Dundee or Glenrothes; an academic teaching university students via the internet; and a books editor. Several of these work from home. It would be impossible now to commute to jobs by public transport; the last regular bus to Cupar was withdrawn in 2014, to be replaced by an irregular subsidised taxibus.

There are some farmers still, although few in number. Land use changes steadily: when Zetland sold up in 1982, there were still soft berries grown on the Flisk estate farms; no longer.[91] We do have alpacas at Higham, however, and as well as cattle and sheep there are perhaps as many horses as there were half a century ago, though they do no farm work. Glenduckie Hill, today in Dutch ownership, has notices dedicating it to 'conservation, educational and enjoyable access objectives' – terms that not even a benign landowner would have used in 1914. Our forests are an investment opportunity, although for recreation rather than for commercial timber. The woods above Ayton have been sold in parcels; for *c*.£45,000 you can own a few acres, shoot, and take your firewood, though you will be 'asked to enter into a covenant to ensure the quiet and peaceful enjoyment of adjoining woodlands and meadows.'[92] Meanwhile, the burned home of the gentleman squire, now rebuilt, has gone for £1.5 million and was made available for hire: you could have it for a wedding, a conference, or a photo shoot.

Some things alter in form if not in substance: Dunbog still frets over energy supplies. Oil-fired heating created a certain cohesion in the form of an oil-buying cooperative, looking for discounts. After the long wait for mains electricity in the 1940s and 50s, today local renewable power is the imperative; three wind turbines

---

[91] Michael Struthers recalls earning £5 a day for berry picking, thinking it a fortune.
[92] www.woodlands.co.uk, January 2014.

DUNBOG GATHERING 2013

overlooking the Tay were refused planning permission, but two others were built at Dunbog, while increasing numbers of homes have solar hot water or photovoltaic (PV) panels, and a PV 'park' above Lindores Loch has been suggested. The glass engraver made his own hydroelectric system out of blue plastic buckets.

At the heart of all this, Dunbog Hall and Dunbog School are together the most visible focus of whatever the community is today, which is not what it was in 1914. The only certainty is more uncertainty; in nearby parishes where schools have closed for lack of children, even modernised halls have struggled to survive. If Dunbog Hall can be flexible, adapting to real, contemporary needs, and if the ceiling doesn't fall down and if the present heating system lasts a bit better than previous versions, then it may be with us for a good while yet. One last major change shows what can happen unexpectedly.

A Community Park

The school – or the community at large – had never had an adequate playing field, and at the time of the Hall Centenary the headteacher Marion Paton was prompting the committee chair (Philip Todd) to do something.

But although there was plenty of neighbouring land, acquiring this would be very expensive, after which it would have to be drained, levelled, landscaped, planted, fenced, equipped, and an extended carpark created. In 2015, National Lottery money paid for a feasibility study. The total cost would be over £100,000.

Clearly this could only be possible with grants, and the obvious grant source was the Scottish Land Fund which supports projects such as the buy-out of entire islands by their communities, or large tracts of open country for rewilding. In order even to apply, however, the Hall Trust would have to be a membership organisation.

So in 2017 the Trust became a Scottish Charitable Incorporated Organisation (SCIO), with everyone living locally offered free membership. Two acres of farmland east of the hall were bought for £32,000, and in September 2017 we celebrated our new ownership. Play equipment was bought with money from two waste recycling firms and by local fundraising; trees and hedging were subsidised by the Woodland Trust. Once the land was prepared, it was re-seeded and closed for eighteen months to allow the grass to grow, while a gathering of families planted holly, rowan and hawthorn along the road side.

In September 2021, we held a Grand Opening and games. The Dunbog Community Park belongs to everyone now, and after school each day many of the parents gather there to talk and wait for their children to come out and play awhile on the swings and climbing frame before going home.

By the gate there is a sign with a few simple rules and requests, the last being the shortest and simplest: Enjoy the park.

BIBLIOGRAPHY & SOURCES

Most of the hall and parish records are now kept at the Fife Council Archives, Bankhead, Glenrothes, where they may be freely consulted. See the Archives website for listings.

Anon. (1866). *The Dunbog Case: report on the Trial of John Bell, Glenduckie.* Cupar, Fife Herald.

Arbuckle, Andrew (2002). *Footsteps in the Furrow*. Ipswich, Old Pond Publishing.

Buchan, Rev. W. S. (1953) *The Parish of Dunbog, its history, kirk and people.* Cupar, J&G Innes.

Callander, Robin F. (1987) *A Pattern of Landownership in Scotland.* Finzean, Haughend Publications.

Devine, Tom M. (1995). *Exploring the Scottish Past: themes in the history of Scottish Society.* East Linton, Tuckwell Press.

Dunbog Parish Hall: legal papers including the feu contract with the Zetland estate (1914), disposition to Dunbog Parish Hall Trust (1952), Deed of Trust (1954) etc. in the care of Pagan Osborne (Solicitors), Cupar.

Dunbog Parish Hall minutes and correspondence (from 1955 et seq.). Fife Council archives.

Dunbog Parish Kirk records (from 1666 et seq.) in the Special Collections of the library of St Andrews University.

Dunbog Parochial Board & Parish Council minutes (1895-1929). Fife Council archives.

Dunbog School Board minute book (1873-1919). Fife Council archives.

Dunbog School log book (1924-1970). Fife Council archives.

Groome, Francis H. (1882-5) *Ordnance Gazetteer of Scotland: A Survey of Scottish Topography, Statistical, Biographical and Historical.* Edinburgh, Thomas C. Jack.

Lamont-Brown, Robert (1988, reprinted 2002). *Fife in History and Legend.* Edinburgh, John Donald.

Leighton, John (1840). *History of the County of Fife.* Glasgow, Joseph Swan.

MacLeod, Robert W. (1996). *Lairds & Farmers in North Fife.* Cupar, privately published.

Pringle, R.H. & Wilkinson E. (1893). *Reports by Mr R Hunter Pringle and Mr Edward Wilkinson on certain selected districts of…Fife.* London, H.M. Stationery Office.

Rowntree, B.S. & Kendall, M (1913). *How the Labourer Lives.* London, T. Nelson.

Smout, T.C. (1986). *A Century of the Scottish People 1830-1950.* London, Collins.

'Statistical Accounts':

– 1791: *A Statistical Account of Scotland ('First Account').* Entry for Dunbog by Rev. Dr Michael Greenlaw of Creich. Edinburgh, W. Creech.

– 1836: *A New Statistical Account of Scotland ('Second Account')* vol.9 (Fife). Entry for Dunbog by Rev. Dr Adam Cairns. Edinburgh, Blackwood.

– 1952: *Third Statistical Account of Scotland ('Third Account')* by Alexander Smith. Edinburgh, Oliver & Boyd.

Taylor, S. & Markus, G. (2010). *The Place Names of Fife* (vol.4). Donington, Shaun Tyas. (These meticulous researches are now available via the 'Fife Place-names' database of Glasgow University.)

Westwood's Parochial Directory for the counties of Fife & Kinross (1st issue 1862, 2nd issue 1866). Cupar, A.Westwood. (Available online.)

NEWSPAPERS: Historical newspaper collection, Cupar Public Library.

MAPS: An important source has been the excellent maps website of the National Library of Scotland, which contains almost all extant maps back to the 17th century. These are digitised and may be examined in close detail.

STATISTICS: The *Know Fife* database assembles a wide range of statistical sources including Census returns, NHS figures, the Scottish Index of Multiple Deprivation, and others.

Other websites consulted include the BBC, Burke's Peerage, Historic Scotland, the Royal Commission on the Ancient and Historical Monuments of Scotland, Canmore (Scotland's archeological record), Scottish Churches, and various pages on the railway, military records, roads, properties, topography and toponyms.

For other information and comments, my thanks go to: Jean Allardice, Andrew Arbuckle, Lynn Brady, Colin Clark (Pagan Osborne, Solicitors), Ron Currie, Andrew Dowsey (Fife Council Archives), Pamela Keen, Lyn Kennedy, Steve Liscoe (Fife Sites & Monuments), Jim McCarthy, Nicholas Morris (Craigrothie Hall), Ken Pithouse, Claire Sillick (RHASS archives), Bill Slee (Hutton Institute, Aberdeen), Jim Stirrat, Michael Struthers, Eric Titterington, and the staff of Cupar Public Library and of St Andrews University Library (Special Collections).

In grateful and respectful memory also of Dennis Currie, Hugh Ingram, Ian Macrae and Davie Thompson.

Printed in Great Britain
by Amazon